A Landscape of Events

Writing **Architecture**

A project of the Anyone Corporation

Earth Moves: The Furnishing of Territories
Bernard Cache, 1995

Architecture as Metaphor: Language, Number, Money
Kojin Karatani, 1995

Differences: Topographies of Contemporary Architecture
Ignasi de Solà-Morales, 1996

Constructions
John Rajchman, 1997

Such Places as Memory
John Hejduk, 1998

Welcome to The Hotel Architecture
Roger Connah, 1998

Fire and Memory: On Architecture and Energy
Luis Fernández-Galiano, 2000

A Landscape of Events
Paul Virilio, 2000

The MIT Press Cambridge, Massachusetts London, England

A Landscape of Events

Paul Virilio
translated by Julie Rose

This work originally appeared in French under the title *Un paysage d'événements*, © 1996 Editions Galilée, Paris.

This book was set in Janson and Franklin Gothic by Graphic Composition, Inc., Athens, Georgia, and was printed and bound in the United States of America.

Library of Congress Cataloging-in-Publication Data

Virilio, Paul.
    [Paysage d'événements. English]
    A landscape of events / Paul Virilio ; translated by Julie Rose.
       p.   cm. — (Writing architecture)
    Includes bibliographical references.
    ISBN 0-262-72034-5 (pbk. : alk. paper)
      I. Title. II. Series.

PQ2682.I586 P3913 2000
844'.914—dc21

00-045210

Events are bigger than people think.
—François Guizot

Contents

Through a series of texts written between 1984 and 1996, P.V., or Paul Virilio, establishes the P.V., the *procès-verbal* of our contemporary society. In French, the "P.V.," as it is referred to colloquially, is an official report, a journal, the minutes of a proceeding, a police report, even a parking or speeding ticket. I have always been struck by the coincidence of these initials. In these essays, P.V. reports on a series of occurrences, incidents, accidents of all sorts—in short, on events—ranging from the World Trade Center bombing to the Gulf War, from the demolition of a social housing project (a French equivalent to Pruitt-Igoe) to the fiftieth anniversary of D Day. The aim is to discuss major transformations in today's society.

Time, rather than space, is the theme of this book: the collapse of time, the acceleration of time, the reversal of time, the simultaneity of all times. Another title for Virilio's *A Landscape of Events* could have been "Mediated Blitzes." Indeed, rarely has a contemporary writer so engaged in an exacerbated analysis of the acceleration of time, to the point where space itself becomes engulfed in time. Space becomes temporal.

Foreword
Bernard Tschumi

For us, as architects, time is spatial because space is what we construct, and time is there to activate these spaces, occasionally to transform them by challenging the perception of their boundaries. Time is what allows us to measure space. But Virilio is somewhere else. When we say that his space becomes temporal, it is because we feel, in reading him, that society has become entirely a function of time, and that duration is really a conjunction of simultaneities.

In "Probable Imminence," the essay that concludes this collection, Virilio notes that "long-term" has become so long that it now exceeds our capacity for statistical prediction, but "short-term" has accelerated so much that immediate decisions are the only decisions ever made. Memory and continuous time are now "academic." If, in the university system, nothing ever seems urgent, in government, on the contrary, everything goes fast; decisions are made in five minutes, a quarter of an hour, an hour. "Long-term" means "a week."

In military terms (and Virilio is passionate about military parallels) one no longer talks about a territory, about a political space that can be enclosed by walls, but about reaction time, which must be cybernated in order to cope with the ever-increasing acceleration of decisions. Here the concept of event takes on its mathematical dimension: an event is any one of all possible occurrences, one of which must happen under stated conditions. According to the theory of probability, the likelihood of such an event happening can even be calculated. Hence I have always felt, as an architect, that it was more exciting to be designing conditions for events than to be conditioning designs. But the architect's means of establishing conditions are primarily spatial.

In Virilio's global temporal space, landscapes become a random network of pure trajectories whose occasional collisions suggest a possible topography: here is a peak, there an abyss. The acceleration of this temporal reality becomes the subject of this book. Each collision is an event relayed by media—political, social, technological. No value judgments here: after all, an event is a kind of accident, one that arises from the unlikely collision of generally uncoordinated vectors. Accidents will happen. Conveyed by media culture, P.V.'s events are less here than now. His definition of the event is less in space than in time. P.V.'s thesis may be simply that time has finally overcome space as our main mode of perception.

For God, *history is a landscape of events.* For Him, nothing really follows sequentially since everything is co-present.

From the smallest fact to the greatest historical event, "there is nothing wonderful before Him."[1] This transhistoric land, so hard to imagine, extends from age to age, from eternity to eternity. There—though where exactly?—generations have been "pouring from times of endless date," in their ever-changing nature—"in their going, in their flowing"—outlined against the horizon of an eternal present.[2]

We can hardly hope to grasp this atemporal perspective, in which before and after coexist, unless we see it as a film. Only, a film in which the sequence shot would constantly keep the beginning and the end in view . . .

A landscape of time in which events suddenly take the place of relief, of vegetation; in which the past and the future loom up together in all their obvious simultaneity; a place where nothing follows on from anything else any more and yet where nothing ever ends, the lack of duration of the perpetual present circumscribing the cycle of history and its repetitions.

Calling Card

But what "relief" are we talking about if the long chain of historical facts and events is linked, for God, to telluric upheavals and landslides? The relief of the truth, meaning, more often than not, of the cruelty of an epoch, the hills and dales of daily life, the usual clumps of habits and commonplaces, the primal forests of the mists of time or the unobstructed clearings of progress?

So many questions that give meaning and direction to the temporal depth of our history remain unspoken, to the point where the threat of "negationism" is now everywhere rampant.

General history or the history of events? From now on, such an academic distinction is no longer merely ambiguous but illusory, for, even if nothing is equivalent, the scale of values of the facts no longer allows simple discrimination between the "general" and the "particular," the "global" and the "local."

Since universal *world time* is gearing up to outstrip the time of erstwhile localities in historical importance, it is now a matter of urgency that we reform the "whole" dimension of general history so as to make way for the "fractal" history of the limited but precisely located event. This is one of the direct and unremarked consequences of throwing out the old, sinister "historical materialism." Otherwise, we should surely be most alarmed by the recent proclamations of a talented young writer: "We are forced to transmit what we know, that is our legacy, *but we share the impotence of those who come after.* This is why I believe we must hold on not only to our memory, *but also to the possibility of forgetting.*" He concludes: "Humanity will banish the twentieth century, the most infamous and murderous of all, from its history; *we should forget it.*"[3]

A landscape has no fixed meaning, no privileged vantage point. It is oriented only by the itinerary of the passerby. But in the essays that follow, it is no longer the big events that make up the fabric of the landscape of time but the myriad incidents, minute facts either overlooked or deliberately ignored.

Here, *the landscape is a passage*—the data transfer accident of the present to the most recent past, a past that goes back some ten or twelve years, a period in which everything has suddenly plunged headlong into a discontinuity that has destroyed the age-old agreement of tenses: the chronaxy that only a little while ago still made sense of history.

From now on, *the only relief is that of the event,* to the point where the temporal horizon is now based exclusively on the crest of the anecdotes and ravages of a present that has no future and whose only legatee seems to be the science of statistics.

If we look for a moment at the reversal that is happening before our very eyes, trend for trend, we see that *fear of the future* has now been outstripped by *fear of the past*, as though the past, far from disappearing, from being erased by the present, continues to weigh it down—worse, to secretly contaminate it.

In this panic reaction, analogous to remorse, it is no longer so much the person, the isolated individual, who is "at fault" but society and the immediate environment.

And so we are already living out *the coexistence of a past not only present but omnipresent*, a past that gets in the way of the future; a coexistence that has stopped being in any way peaceful since nuclear deterrence is itself over and done with and all kinds of threats proliferate at leisure.

Indeed, when you run into an obstacle, an insuperable barrier, the impact makes you recoil. This is evidently what has just happened; *history has just crashed into the wall of time*, the barrier of this "real time" that corresponds to a cosmological constant, the speed of light in a vacuum.

Tracking out, *the recession of history entails the retreat of knowledge, the retirement of progress.* Suddenly, everything is escaping: ethical and political ideals, the durability of societies and the stability of population demographics.

To observe this sudden unfolding of time in which not only history is accelerating, as before, but also its *reality*, we need to adopt the perspective of Sirius and step back, get our distance to avoid the contemporary myopia of the media age.

Walter Benjamin once wrote, "A Klee painting named 'Angelus Novus' shows an angel *looking as though he is about to move away from something he is fixedly contemplating.* His eyes are staring, his mouth is open, his wings are spread. This is how one pictures the angel of history. *His face is turned toward the past.* Where we perceive a chain of events, *he sees a single catastrophe* which keeps piling wreckage upon wreckage and hurls it at his feet."[4]

Today this theological vision no longer belongs to the angel of history. It has become the vision of each and every one of us.

From now on, the acceleration of the reality of time causes revulsion at the being-here-present. Like fright, which results in the body's retreat, evaporation of hope in the future causes us to regress, inducing permanent resentment.

The work that follows is devoted to this radical reversal in perspective. It is halfway between an essay and a narrative in which a series of atypical events succeed each other over the course of only a dozen or so years; events whose scope has escaped the theorists as much as the historians of the moment.

P.V.

A Landscape of Events

Some enchanted evening,
the future is called the past.
—Louis Aragon

The false day of technoculture rightly sprang up out of those vast death traps that the first great cities of the industrial world turned into at night. Hell without the fire, with their murderous princes and gutter princesses stepping out in the mud, absolute squalor of a shady populace devoted unstintingly to doing evil.

The police never risked venturing into the strange landscapes of that nocturnal no-man's-land, *not so much enchanted as damned*, except in groups—until the moment police lieutenant Gabriel Nicolas de La Reynie put an end to that dark night by inventing "lighting inspectors" to reassure the Parisian public, and especially to encourage them to go out and enjoy themselves at night.[1]

One
The Big Night

When La Reynie quit his post as police chief in 1697, there were 6,500 street lamps democratically lighting up the capital. The Englishman Joseph Lister, comparing the "City of Light" to London, which was not yet so privileged, wrote, "The streets of Paris are ablaze all through winter and even of a full moon."

The cess of majesty
Dies not alone, but like a gulf doth draw
What's near it with it.[2]

King Sun no longer orchestrated time in town; sunrise and sunset lost their purpose. In the Age of Enlightenment, that rhythmic duality that is at the beginning of everything found itself eliminated from our physiology and our consciousness. Like newborn babes, we were to mistake night for day. Night was to be exorcised, dragged unsuspectingly not into the light of day but under the streetlights.

The man of Creation (of Genesis), the man of the rural world, would gradually yield to the *perverted peasant* of urban prostitution.

The extraterritoriality of nightlife would absorb a short and seasonal diurnal life. Later, the surrealists would again salute this great transmutation of "the moon into green cheese," the gold of day having turned to lead and artificial night bursting before *our newly anointed eyes.*

Necessity is the mother of invention, as the logicians used to say. And it is precisely over their necessity that the boundless possibilities of a technoculture eaten up by its noctambulism are today stumbling.

The sun that never set on the empire of Charles the Fifth will never rise over the coming empire of digital time.

Days that once, forty years ago, spread out over the whole planet, with just a few hours' time difference, have been replaced by the supplementary and simulated days of screens, consoles, and other "night tables," which will take over completely this time from those days of once-diurnal activities. After the fields and the forests, the cities and suburbs will be evacuated of work and social intercourse; after the space of the countryside, urban space will be destroyed.

The web of multimedia—that ever-watchful spider— will be merely a grotesque caricature of the global village of Marshall McLuhan, who will someday look like the bucolic Jean-Jacques Rousseau of digital times. A bit like the architects of those so-called Radiant Cities, who dreamed of building ideal towns but in the end made only ghettos, followed shortly by "free zones." Imagining that they could adapt the transparent models of "enlightened society" to the peoples of Babel, they managed only to accommodate the transterritoriality of nighttime, as others before them had done in red light districts known as *tolerant neighborhoods!*[3] The so-called bedroom communities quite naturally becoming, over the years, no-go areas always on the go, in an absolute reversal of biological cycles, with inhabitants dozing by day, awake at night, goaded sporadically by free radio calls for looting, destruction, hate, and gratuitous murder . . . the latest arrivals shoving out their predecessors with a good dose of violence.

After the great massacre of the American Indians by the WASPs, the Italians expel the WASPs, the blacks the Italians, the Hispanics the blacks, etc. In the United States, overcrowded no-go areas are now spreading so fast that certain ethnic groups, having conquered vast urban territories, are now demanding independence—like the inhabitants of the San Fernando Valley (1.6 million strong) who consider they have been exploited by the rest of the city of Los Angeles and so are considering secession, with the approval of the Senate of California. Others, more ambitious, are claiming the whole of certain American states where they reckon they are the majority . . .

Whatever the case may be, it is estimated that between now and the end of the millennium, 30 percent of the population will take shelter in *cities of refuge* removed from the escheated megalopolises: *priva-topias*, much like entrenched camps, protecting the comfortable existence, the life and goods, of the privileged sons and daughters of technoliberalism on hostile and fragmented territory.

"You can't live in New York during the day, you can only live here at night," filmmaker Abel Ferrara recently told a journalist.

No doubt this is why a new medicine has been freely available in the United States for the past few years: *mela-*

tonin. The immense popular success of melatonin ultimately recalls the success of dark glasses at the beginning of the century. "One can take to dark glasses the way one takes to tobacco or alcohol," noted Aldous Huxley apropos those optical instruments paradoxically *designed for you not to see* the light of the sun and to provide the sensation of going unnoticed in broad daylight as though it were night. Dark glasses were adopted very early on by both movie stars and torturers.

As for this famous melatonin, Professor Jean-Pierre Collin reminds us that *it is produced naturally by all vertebrates during the nocturnal phase of their biological clocks:* "Melatonin is a hormone directly secreted by the pineal gland and transported by the bloodstream. It serves as a *temporal landmark* as much in relation to the twenty-four hour cycle as to the course of the yearly cycle. We might think of it as a *molecule for adapting to one's surroundings.*"

Thanks to the untimely use of this substance, night and day become equivalent; we no longer know *physiologically* where night ends and day begins, what the difference is between here and there, for melatonin takes on the job of filling in the last remaining gaps, erasing distinctions, compensating for our optical transgressions, the nuisance of jet lag.

Born of the precariousness of diurnal life and the dreams of the gangster Bugsy Siegal, Las Vegas is evidently shaping up as the ultimate "City of Light." Arriving at night, you have the impression of entering an electrical power station going full bore. During the day, the set changes and you realize that what Las Vegas really resembles is one of those ghost towns you sometimes come across in the vast wastelands of America. A long central avenue, the Strip, is bordered by caricatures of buildings, and every year twenty-two million insomniac visitors line up to take their turn in the endless night of the windowless *slot-machine halls* of luxury hotel casinos.

The beam of light projected by the Luxor from the top of its fifty-five stories is, we are told, the most powerful on the planet. Apparently you can see it even from the moon.

"Some enchanted evening, the future is called the past," wrote Louis Aragon. Reversal occupied Hannah Arendt as well, in her 1971 *The Life of the Mind*: "The quest for meaning, which relentlessly dissolves and examines anew all accepted doctrines and rules, can at any moment turn against itself, produce a *reversal of the old values*, and declare these contraries to be *new values*." Arendt gives as an example in the criminal realm the reversal of "Thou shalt not kill" in Nazi Germany.

But Arendt hastens to add that, before Hitler, "this is what Nietzsche did when he reversed Platonism, *forgetting that a reversed Plato is still Plato*, or what Marx did when he turned Hegel upside down, *producing a strictly Hegelian system of history in the process*."[4]

Later, the situationist Guy Debord was to remark, "We didn't try to find the formula for *overthrowing the world* in books *but by roaming around*."

And there is the difference between the old "teachers of the masses," studiously installed at their desks, under a lamp, and the professional browsers of the transportation and transmission revolution—physical transport and optical transport—specialists in time differences, revolutionary jet-setters amidst a general roaming in which the *dislocation* of the real world derives spontaneously from the *delocalization* and accelerated displacement of bodies (dislocate is from the Latin, *dislocare:* to move about, displace).

Apotheosis of enlightenment, journey to the end of night: between Hannah Arendt taking stock, at the end of a tormented life, of a "flash-frozen" body of thought that turns its back on the course of historical time, and the words of Guy

Debord, what stands out is that the *Big Night so long awaited* has arrived, if only because our perception of the world has imploded.

At the end of the nineteenth century, Edgar Degas, painter and lover of the camera obscura, was thus able to tell us a great deal more about future times than his contemporary philosophers and theorists, Marx and Nietzsche—with, for instance, a formula so far ahead of its time that it seemed meaningless then: "By freeing itself from Nature's tyranny, art sums itself up rather than extends itself."

"To free oneself"—in other words, to be unhampered, to be free in one's movements—is, as we know, a purely negative action. As for "Nature," like Villiers de l'Isle-Adam's hero Axël, *we have never met the dame!*

On the other hand, if we swap *natural light* for that vague term *nature*, it is easier to see that by freeing ourselves from natural lighting (from cosmological time), we have, in just over two centuries, come to resemble moles roaming in a *beam of light*, moles whose view of the world does not indeed amount to much. *You learn by looking*, they say. Well, we really have unlearned a lot in this dazzling period that has seen such an impressive number of converts to Degas's precept—and not just in the area of the traditional arts.

So we would no more be able to stop "progress" than resolve the nebulosity of extraterrestrial time—the pathetic progress of an *aesthetics of disappearance* whose first moral expressions, the most spontaneous, the most obvious, have included historical nihilism and negationism.

And yet it would be an adept of transparent architecture, Mies van der Rohe, who would have the last word, so to speak, with his dizzying and necessarily brief formula: Less is more.

The formula for *overthrowing the world* that Debord sought in the wild excesses of a general roaming had long been found by our architect somewhere between the tragedy of Dessau and Chicago: *it was the very act of overthrowing*.

Arendt's corrupted master, Heidegger, a witness to Hitler's *totale Mobilmachung*, which he advocated, was perfectly comfortable writing, in 1938: "However far our epoch has taken the taste for mobility, one cannot claim that a movement without goal or direction is sufficient in itself."

But that was not counting on the lapidary *Diktat* of Mies van der Rohe, that modern golden rule that opened us up to the paradoxical logic of a new era. Less is more, from the countdown to the speed record, from cubism to nuclear disintegration, from consumerism to computer science, from aerodynamics to the anorexia of top models, from technoliberalism to the cyber, from deforestation to the great ethnic massacres.

"All the signs of the decline of social life, of politics, of civilian life, must be interpreted positively as signs of the coming of the cyber," Michael Heim, a distant California disciple of Heidegger, recently wrote. "It is true," Heim goes on to say, "that in entering cyberspace we risk abandoning a part of the population to its fate, but technoculture is our destiny."[5]

More realistic advocates of less is more, Nicholas Negroponte of MIT and John Perry Barlow, president of the Electronic Frontier Foundation, specify for their part: "We have entered the digital age, the age of a universal network with no one in charge, no president, no chief. . . . Because of the network's decentralized structure, it will in any case be impossible to censor it without banning the telephone! And this is a good thing, for cybernetic space should reflect *a society of individuals* and in no case become the plaything of government!"[6]

The absolute paradox of a society of individuals "with no one in charge, no law, no chief" is already looming in the nocturnal splitting off of anational and asocial urban fringes that keep growing at the expense of the older, historic quarters—and also with the recent creation of priva-topias in America or the Japanese "side-by-side" city projects.

"The world is one and common to those who are awake, but everybody who is asleep turns away to his own," Heraclitus once said. After the disastrous attempts at new lifestyles in the communes of the 1960s, the mad expansion of nocturnal transterritoriality was bound to wind up in an *oneiric individualism* of the sort Plato showed us in the *Republic*. A quasi-natural way out for a lapsed democratic ideal; a state halfway between democracy and the tyrannies to come, the essentially criminal world of nonlaw: "When he was still democratically minded and under the influence of the laws and his father, they [immoral attitudes] only appeared in dreams; but under the tyranny of the master-passion, he becomes in reality what he was once only occasionally in his dreams, and there's nothing, no murder, no outrage however terrible, no unfit food, from which he will shrink."[7]

We might note further that, for fifty years or so, social connotations have been progressively eliminated from everyday language.

And so, alongside the admirable work done by hospitals in repair and reeducation, the different media have engaged in a public relations rehabilitation of disability and certain diseases that is far from innocent. The term *mental illness*, for instance, is no longer heard. It used to mean "a mental disturbance involving an inaptitude for living in society." The term *alienist* for psychiatrist has also disappeared, along with *mental asylum*—or *madhouse*—which then discreetly turned into *psychiatric hospital*. The *clinical* took over from the *social* and from a type of denial often linked to a form of delirium known as *delusions of grandeur* in which subjects arrogate to themselves exceptional dimensions and powers—physical, intellectual, sexual, professional, etc.

In retrospect, we might wonder if it hadn't become a bit awkward putting out of circulation individuals clinically conforming to the norms of postindustrial society, to those *delusions of grandeur* that technomarketing was gearing up to satisfy by placing at everyone's disposal an impressive number of *virtual devices*—and totally autonomous devices, at that.

"The age of giants is over," André Malraux declared, evoking the careers of the "great men" who had disappeared (Napoleon, Churchill, de Gaulle). And good riddance, for a whole host of dwarfs could then deck themselves out on the cheap with the attributes of power once reserved exclusively for wildly extravagant potentates, deified tyrants, and other "masters of the universe."

"Dreams take no account of the world's dimensions," writes Graham Greene. "In dreams a puddle can contain a continent, a copse of trees stretch to the ends of the earth."

With the new means of transportation and transmission, the new virtual tools, *it is man who gives himself wildly extravagant dimensions and the earth that reveals its limits.*

And so it has been announced that the American billionaire Donald Trump, a real estate speculator converted to gambling and casinos, will shortly take part in a "supersonic golf tournament." The performance is to take place on three different continents on one and the same day: on 3 August 1996, the sixty participants will be able to putt successively in Marrakech (Africa), Shannon (Europe), and Atlantic City (United States). Thanks to the chartering of a special Concorde, three continents are reduced to the size of a golf course and the confines of the earth to those of a green.

Faced with feats of that order, we might ask ourselves about these new dimensions that are likely to be reduced to nothing at this end of the millennium by a technoculture that eludes law and custom a bit more every day (do we punish a machine, which by definition is innocent?).

The answer, though, awaits us in those great mass graves that our century would like to forget. Bodies are no longer the ultimate matter, our skin the final frontier, our consciences the training ground for a world being turned on its head. The new limits are now to be found *beyond*, in otherwise transcendent realms.

Let's go back to what Hannah Arendt, that expert in nihilism, had to say regarding this "reversal of the old values" which are immediately declared to be "new values" and adopted as such. We discover that Hitler's *commandment to kill*, cynically playing on Judeo-Christian morality, is then superseded by a *ban on surviving*, at least spiritually. A new edict daily relayed by the mass media, which now target God himself.

Having systematically exhausted daytime and time on earth with the aid of a bit of acceleration, why not indeed now deny eternity?[8]

A short time ago I ran into a friend who looked very troubled. Her twenty-year-old daughter had just died of a cerebral hemorrhage.

"But she was very healthy," she told me, as though apologizing for some defect. After a long pause, she added, on a happier note: "Anyway, she donated her organs and they've all taken well!"

In the end, the woman was able to forget her daughter's body without too much trouble, since that *flesh of her flesh*, dispersed like so many unhoped-for fetuses, had found itself back *in vivo*, propelled on new and unconscious journeys.

After all, her daughter had not really left the world into which my friend had brought her, so surely now there would be no real difference between intrauterine darkness and the darkness of this world where her child had, supposedly, *seen the light of day* twenty years earlier?

15 May 1996

I have already forgotten the sixth of June 1994. The only thing I remember is that red parachute that didn't open properly and went down near Sainte-Mère-Eglise, like a bad omen . . . Or the veteran who bent down to collect some sand on the beach of Omaha . . . Already the memory of this fiftieth-anniversary "telelanding," destined to perpetuate the memory of the sixth of June 1944, is fading.

As always, the strange cathode skylight has fulfilled its function of digesting the event, the averred fact; the defeat has been consummated: we will talk no more of the Battle of Normandy, except in history books.

Despite the recent proliferation of "museums of the landings," all of that will disappear, has already disappeared, in the industrialization of forgetting, with the small screen as machine tool. If the battlefield was still a field of perception for combatants of both camps at the time of the assault on the beaches of Normandy, its commemoration half a century later will have been merely a field of deep disappointment for the blasé televiewer.

Two
The Avant-Garde of Forgetting

In the manner of Alzheimer's disease, television destroys our past feelings. Viewed from the present, D Day has shriveled in a speeded-up perspective effect that the small screen accentuates. While the illustrated history book evokes the mental imagery of real or emblematic memories, the television monitor collapses memory's close-ups and cancels the coherence of our fleeting impressions. It is hardly an accident, after all, that the Italian neo-fascist leader Gianfranco Fini, profiting from such amnesia, recently told a journalist from *La Stampa:*

"I wonder if D Day, with the American landing, isn't also the day Europe lost its cultural identity."

Fifty years on, with victory metamorphosing into defeat, the job of disinformation is thus done, a piece of deception achieved by both politics and the media.

But let's retrace our steps, let's go back over contemporary history one last time before we hand it over completely to the historians. At dawn on the sixth of June 1944, Robert Capa embarked on a landing craft with three other accredited photographers to cover the "longest day," disembarking with the Marines at Omaha Beach. At the risk of his life, Capa managed to take four rolls of film and send them to the director of photography of *Life* magazine, John Morris, in London. The films were excellent but an unfortunate handling error in the laboratory made them unusable, except for eleven shots miraculously saved from the disaster. The most famous of these was published immediately, with an apology cautioning readers that *if this shot was a bit blurred, it was because Robert Capa had moved while he was shooting!*

Half a century later, it is no longer the photographer that moves but the "politico-media" interpretation, and Italy welcomes the American president in the presence of fascist—sorry, postfascist—ministers. Suddenly revisited by the transalpine media, the history of Europe no longer even stammers out an apology; it completely retracts.

In the age of the great battles of the past, as you will recall, there were the great plains of the East lending themselves to multiethnic invasions. Then there were the great beaches of the West conducive to landings, to the liberation of a continent. Tomorrow, have no fear, there will be the great time slots for the invasion of the multimedia, with their TV station heads, their *condottieri*, and their great orators able to whip the enthralled crowds into a frenzy.

I remember the fortieth anniversary of the landing in 1984, Orwell's year. I can still see Ronald Reagan giving a Cold War speech at Pointe du Hoc and then accompanying his wife, Nancy, on a visit to the German bunkers once conquered by the Rangers.

I also remember, some twenty years earlier, the filming of *The Longest Day* at that same Pointe du Hoc. Sitting in the shade of the powerful command post of the Longues battery, made up with fresh camouflage paint for the occasion, I can see the squadrons simulating the aerial support once given to the Rangers as they stormed the Norman cliffs.

With set and reality mixed up, in film as on television, I have to go back further still into the past to try to finally get to the truth. It is evening, dusk is gathering over the countryside around Nantes, some three hundred kilometers from the Normandy front.

Reflected by the upper layers of the atmosphere of the summer of 1944, the dull and distant sound of the battle of the Falaise Pocket reaches me, falling out of the sky like some cosmic phenomenon. I can still hear it, muffled by the density of the half-century gone by.

In the end, this is *the truth*, a truth transmitted not via the Hertzian waves of some "information tool" but by the reflection of sound off clouds, a reflection that strangely increases their reach. Here, moreover, is the scientific explanation of this little-understood phenomenon: "The firing of cannons or the explosion of high-powered bombs has given rise to all sorts of meteorological observations for some little time now, and curious claims have been made about the propagation of sound. When the Austrian cannons fired on Antwerp, for instance, it was noted that within a radius of sixty to eighty kilometers—the skip zone—the noise of the detonations was not perceived, whereas it was heard much farther away, along the north coast of the Netherlands. This is easily explained if one bears in mind the discontinuity produced in the earth's atmosphere at an altitude of around eighty kilometers, where there is a less dense layer of hydrogen. Sound is reflected off this layer and, in descending to earth, reaches the second 'noise zone.' This is what the meteorologists call an *atmospheric echo*."

With this extract from the Hachette almanac for 1916, we can certainly better measure the nature of the propagation of sound information and its vagaries. But where does this leave us today with the—artificial—propagation of audiovisual information and its "shadow areas" of poor reception?

Listen to Larry King, star CNN anchor assigned to Normandy to cover the events of the fiftieth anniversary of the landing: "Thanks to TV, young people have undoubtedly learned more than in school. They have understood that it was a just cause. It was a great lesson of history, whose emotional aspect *was magnified by the fact that there were still people around to bear witness*."[1]

That says it all. When there are no longer any witnesses, there is no longer any memory and television's shadow area stretches to infinity.

Thirty years ago, the Empire Theater in Paris showed a very long newsreel, nearly ten hours' worth. If I remember rightly, its title was *Forty Years of History*.

I got there early in the morning with a dozen pals and we promptly took over a whole row of seats, loaded up as we were with sandwiches, thermoses of coffee, and bottles of beer. This was the end of the sixties; it was not yet the "end of history," but it was already the end of a world that had taken us on quite a trip, here and there; in any case, far from reality. At the time, Joseph Losey's *The Damned* was my favorite film, with its cult phrase, "It's too late to have a private life." For a whole day, with short intermissions, we saw the first "prewar," the First World War, the interwar years, the

Second World War, and finally *our own postwar* parading past. We didn't give a damn about Sarajevo. As for the speeches booming from the Reichstag, we already knew them through Charlie Chaplin's parodies . . . No, what really thrilled us was to see the vehicles, the women's frocks and evening attire, the hats of the officials, transformed before our very eyes. Also the mutation of the buildings as the twenties unfolded, the slow-motion sequences and the coming of sound to film . . . We looked on all this as a traveling shot forty years long. As in a slow-motion film in which you see plants growing, buds developing, flowers unfolding, and petals falling, we could feel Hitler growing beneath the Kronprinz and the stratospheric rockets flying off beneath Georges Guynemer's plane.

It wasn't history, not really a documentary. For us it was a sort of vision of the great circus of Time, of this *landscape of events* that God alone can contemplate.

18 June 1994

The attack on the World Trade Center is the first of the post–Cold War. No matter who is responsible, it ushers in a new era of terrorism having nothing in common with the explosions that regularly rock Ireland or England.

Indeed, the outstanding feature of the attack is that it was seriously intended to bring down the World Trade Center building; in other words, to bring about the deaths of tens of thousands of innocent people. In the manner of a massive aerial bombardment, this single bomb, made of several hundred kilos of explosives placed at the building's very foundations, could have caused the collapse of a tower four hundred meters high. So it is not a matter of a simple remake of the film *Towering Inferno*, as the image-conscious media like to keep saying, but much more of a strategic event confirming for us all *the change in the military order of this fin-de-siècle.*

As the bombs of Hiroshima and Nagasaki, in their day, signaled a new era for war, the explosive van in New York illustrates the mutation of terrorism.

Three
Delirious New York

Inaugurated by the collapse of the Berlin Wall and even more by the Gulf War, the end of the age of nuclear deterrence is today confirmed by the civil war in the former Yugoslavia but also by this luckily abortive attempt to bring down the New York tower.

Driven to a frightening escalation by the uncertainties of American foreign policy, and especially by the question mark hanging over young President Clinton's capacity to implement it—will he turn out to be a Kennedy or a Carter?—the enemies of Western policies are putting the adversary to the test! Though we too often forget, military intervention has not hung back waiting for the recent resolutions of the UN Security Council, with their "humanitarian" dimension. The gunboat diplomacy of colonialism has long since been thoroughly revived by terrorist action, the offensive intervention of commandos more or less controlled by certain states as well as the fledgling power of narco-capitalism.

With the New York bomb, we thus find ourselves faced with the latest escalation in the kind of military-political action that is based simultaneously on a limited number of actors and guaranteed media coverage. It has reached the point where soon, if we don't look out, a single man may well be able to bring about disasters that were once, not long ago, the province of a naval or air force squadron.

Indeed, for some time the miniaturization of charges and advances in the chemistry of detonation have been promoting a previously unimaginable equation: One man = Total war.

At the very moment that the United Nations is hoping to reestablish an international tribunal to try the authors of war crimes, it is equally urgent to severely punish terrorist practices, no matter what their source; otherwise we will look on, powerless, as this type of "economical" operation suddenly proliferates, capable as it is of inflicting incredible damage not only on the innocent victims but also, and especially, on democracy.

After the age of the *balance of terror*, which lasted some forty years, the *age of imbalance* is upon us. The historic attack on the World Trade Center marks its beginning. A veritable big bang, this criminal act cannot continue to be downplayed for fear of causing panic for the inhabitants of the great metropolises. Indeed, there is no point in waiting for the future "nuclear terrorism" to begin, if the states responsible or those more or less controllable organizations are already daring to take such action: trying to bring down one of the tallest buildings in the world to express their differences or their political opposition, regardless of whether they kill twenty or thirty thousand people in the process. It is urgent that we protect ourselves effectively at the very moment that the American media are set to launch the Military Channel, which will broadcast documentaries and serials about war, weapons, and explosives twenty-four hours a day!

After New York on February 2, it was Bombay on March 13 and Calcutta four days later, where new charges were exploded with the intention of destroying the stock exchange of India's economic capital and three buildings in the commercial district of Bow Bazaar, not far from the center of the country's former colonial capital.

If we add to this the IRA's recent attack on the City of London, we find ourselves faced with a large-scale offensive from the proponents of terror. Even if there are clearly different causes and objectives involved, affecting regions with no apparent connection, no one can deny the catalogue of disasters that are today striking the world's great strategic centers.

In the United States, the World Trade Center is, as we know, an economic nerve center; the same goes for the Bombay Stock Exchange or the City of London, and the Bow Bazaar of Calcutta is likewise an important business mecca in India.

Three hundred dead in Bombay and close to a thousand seriously injured, fifty dead in Calcutta and close to a hundred injured . . . Even though there were no more than five dead and ten seriously injured in New York, the terrorist dimension of such bomb attacks no longer has anything in common with the political petty crime of recent years. The perpetrators are determined not merely to settle the argument with guns now, but to try to devastate the major cities of the world marketplace.

We now find ourselves faced with a model of "organized terrorism," and just as we speak of organized crime as opposed to classic petty crime in matters of public safety, we must get used to distinguishing between the "petty terror-ism" of the age of nuclear deterrence and this terrorism that, with the end of the Cold War, inaugurates the age of nuclear proliferation.

Yet we need to review the recent revolution in weapons systems to interpret a mutation that is qualitative as well as quantitative. From the beginning of the nineties and par-ticularly with the war in the Persian Gulf, we have seen the strategic emergence of "communications weapons" that have superseded the traditional supremacy of "weapons of destruction" and "weapons of obstruction"—in other words, the duel of arms and armor.

After the three military fronts of land, sea, and air, we are seeing the gradual buildup of a fourth front: that of the power of information.

Let's not forget that international terrorism is insepa-rable from this *media front* and that terrorist attacks make sense and have political value only because of the televised publicity they invariably have at their disposal. With the telegenic quality of such atrocities constantly reinforcing their evocative power, certain countries, such as the former Soviet Union and Italy, have even gone as far as placing a blanket ban on media coverage of the worst terrorist atroci-ties (along with accidents).

If the miniaturization of destructive power can now al-low a single man or a small commando unit to inflict damage similar to that of a broad-based military operation, it goes without saying that the mass war of the armies of yore risks being supplanted by some mass killer using the impact of the mass media to exert maximum pressure on international public opinion.

What is remarkable here is that the sudden proliferation of the "molecular" terror of traditional explosives—in antici-pation of the proliferation of "nuclear" terror—is accompa-nied by a growing impoverishment of war. We are going back to the conflicts of the fifteenth century, to the *condottieri* and the great bands of brigands that once plundered the European countryside in the days of private wars . . . In the end, you don't need much money if you have enough charisma, religious or otherwise, to buy a band of paramilitary assassins.

This is what we see happening today, as much in the Balkans as in Medellín or Burma, within the golden triangle of drugs—not to mention the various mafias in Russia and elsewhere.

Note by way of provisional conclusion that the attack on the World Trade Center is testimony to the clever combination of a strong symbolic dimension and an urban demolition capability involving only a small number of individuals who used a delivery van to deliver terror. In the days of cruise missiles and the most sophisticated nuclear weapons carriers, you have to admit that this is a striking example of political economy!

30 March 1993

> *We can do with the new weapons what we thought we*
> *could only do with nuclear weapons.*
> —*Colin Powell*

A bit like in the Magritte painting titled *L'Anniversaire*, an enormous block hangs in the air clouding the horizon of New Year 1992, that of a war forgotten with the extinguishing of the last fires in Kuwait's oil wells.

Already lost to sight, the Gulf War is receding into the vacuum of consciousness at the speed of the meteorite that apparently came within a hair's breadth of the earth's surface twelve months ago . . .

Overexposed for one hundred long days, this conflict has finally suffered the same fate as *the news.* The first televisual war, the war of the Persian Gulf has not escaped the law of the genre: *now you see it, now you don't.* It is enough to make you think the electronic process known as *image compression,* which allows information to be stored, has promoted the compression of history and finally the disappearance of the event!

Four

The Imbalance of Terror

A war in two dimensions—plus a third, the dimension of time, of the real time of televised broadcasts—a world war in miniature perceived via the intermediary of the screen, the Gulf War is inseparable from its cathodic framing, to the point where it only subsists afterward in the memory of those video cassettes now on sale alongside war games and the Nintendo series.

Where the cunning chronology of the history books used to cut and paste the facts, from the wars of antiquity to the war of 1939–1945, the careful framing of the screen and the moment of broadcast today reorganize the narrative of a conflict too quick to be publicly analyzed. As for those—journalists or diplomats—who still believe that you should wait before writing history, they are living in the wrong century!

How can we in fact analyze, in historical terms, *the miniaturization of this war*, a total war in which local space disappeared in a global and instantaneous military management operation?

How can we explain, in all seriousness, a conflict so dense and especially so short, in which communications weapons used in intelligence as well as telerobotics took precedence over weapons of mass destruction?

Instead of circumscribing the "real space" of battle, as in the old days, they have this time rigorously reduced and controlled the "real time" of confrontation.

With erstwhile geostrategy itself having shifted to the infinitesimal scale of electromagnetism, tomorrow's historian will have to try above all to get to know the wave function of the weapons systems, the applications of the Hertzian devices, before claiming to understand anything about their outcomes!

A reduced model of large-scale confrontation, the Gulf War possesses the enigmatic characteristics of a mock-up in relation to the "real object" it is supposed to represent. A mock-up of the Strategic Defense Initiative, hatched by Ronald Reagan as early as 1983, the Gulf War seven years later was at once a promotional war for the victorious American armaments and an experimental war: a *strategic experiment* in which the fate of Kuwait mattered less than the practical results of a test carried out over the smallest possible surface area in the shortest amount of time. Whence the primary importance of the various tools of mass communication, capable of revealing this spectacle to the world in what amounts to an all-out advertising campaign.

Not only has modern man been able to miniaturize motors, machines, and the microprocessors in them; he has just made war minuscule too. Having gotten used for the last twenty years or so to the shrinking of an earth *seen from space*, man now knows how to reduce to nothing (or nearly so) a whole world war!

"The best way to reflect infinity is to reflect it in some tiny thing; *the temptation of the West is the small format*," the Italian writer Pietro Citati recently claimed. In making total war "intensive" and no longer "extensive," postmodern man has now even managed to reduce the format of violence to its simplest expression: *an image*.

The panorama of titanic battles is suddenly reduced to the format of the small screen. Total war, once geophysical, becomes *microphysical*. An attraction to miniaturization has surely been a constant of scientific thought and its lapidary formulae, such as $E = mc^2$; a constant of those "experimental" sciences that have ended up making war "elementary"—in other words, atomic.

Another perspective has emerged that confirms this observation: with the recent decline in the traditional military notions of *offensive* and *defensive*, following on from the loss of supremacy of the army and specifically of ground forces, the dialectic of combat waged on the battlefield has now vanished, the instantaneity and ubiquity of the different means of action having completely distorted the geostrategic notions of *front* and *rear*, just as they have distorted the *chronostrategic* notions of *pre-* and *postwar*.

While the revolution in physical transportation has just been coupled with that in microphysical transmission, we are already seeing the beginnings of a third revolution: the *transplantation* revolution, thanks to the process of grafting, implanting interactive components in programmed automatons such as the Tomahawk cruise missile, used profusely during the Gulf War. Not content to reduce to nothing the time lapse necessary for action, they are now introducing instantaneous tools of perception and decision-

making right inside the mechanisms of weapons, using remote control in real time. This does away with the classic
distinction between *inside* and *outside* and, in doing so, occa-
sions the discreet fusion of the *external* and *internal space* of
the machine . . . Real war is thus no longer conducted solely
on the geographic field of action but, initially and essentially, in the absence of field, inside the organs of the missile.
The real space of the weapon's technical configuration
yielding to the primacy of the real time of measures said to
be *interactive.*

Whence those famous countermeasures that attack, so
to speak, the integrated circuits of enemy weaponry, and to
which the usual notions of offensive and defensive no longer
apply: the instantaneity of the interaction of electromagnetic
beams no longer participating in the strategic or tactical
mechanisms of action and reaction.

From that moment, the law of least effort, so crucial in
any technical system, itself becomes outmoded, for, paradoxically, it is the lack of any humanly perceptible action that
wins out over the customary activity of attack or defense:
data *input* and *output* replace the usual notions of fight or
flight, as we have seen notably with the problems posed by
computer viruses.

With smart weapons systems, such as the Patriot antimissile, what is essentially involved is a *weapons ecosystem* that
bears absolutely no relation to the environment in which the
conflict unfolds. In such extreme conditions, how can we
hope for long to distinguish between *actor* and *spectator, soldier* and *civilian?* Combining and, indeed, confusing information systems with systems for controlling public opinion
become inevitable.

Finally, in this exotic conflict in which the supremacy of
orbital intelligence showed itself to be total, the actor-
spectators witnessed the use of the first *pure weapons* in history. Weapons that paralyze the opponent less through their

devastating power than by *prohibiting all military action of any scope.* A microconflict in which wiping out the enemy and its commander-in-chief or occupying its territory was no longer required for victory.

For more than forty years, East-West deterrence gave credence to the idea of a pure war, a war uncontaminated by any actual engagement, since the atomic bomb was supposed to rule out the horror of a world war. The end of the Cold War in turn involves the emergence of a new concept: that of *pure weapons*, whose use would recuperate what was essential to the terrorizing psychological achievements of the age of nuclear deterrence. These weapons are said to be capable of producing the same results, paralyzing the enemy and rendering their command inert, no longer thanks to the performance of a projectile carrying a terrifying explosive but to the rapidity and extreme precision of its delivery—and this as much in the sighting or surveillance of enemy movements as in the *selectiveness and stealth* of the strike.

A strike not unrelated to the treatment of a malignant tumor by laser irradiation, an operation that even makes the intervention of a scalpel unnecessary; a strike so effective and so painless that it barely changes the habits of the patient, who is then free to go about his or her business as though nothing has happened.

Whence also the importance of strictly limiting operations to a minuscule area and to the shortest possible time, so short that the most watchful observers (journalists and others) *would never see a thing!*

Whence also the urgency of drastically framing images as "consumer" information, which, if we are not careful, will soon impose the gradual militarization not only of scientific knowledge, which has already happened with the flourishing of the military-industrial complex, but of *the very sources of general information.* Information which, in the age of the absolute supremacy of "selective weapons of communication," can no longer remain open for long to criticism via the plurality of expression of mass communication tools. In the very near future, we can expect to see the emergence of a veritable *military-information complex* whose initial symptoms will have been the role of CNN and the pool of journalists directly controlled by the Pentagon during the Gulf War.

More than ten years ago, the defense bodies of the "free world"—in France, notably those centered around the army information service directed by General Pinatel—were already setting up systems for close media surveillance, to avoid, so they said, the ravages of terrorist acts that played on their media coverage. In the United States, the proceedings begun by General Westmoreland against CBS in 1984–1985 highlighted the disastrous political fallout from a news system free to reveal the most sordid aspects of a conflict like the Vietnam War (the Mylai massacre, soldiers on drugs, etc.). With the Persian Gulf affair, as with the military intervention on the island of Grenada and more recently in Panama, the issue of control of the media environment became an absolute priority for the American high command![1]

Far from wanting to dramatize an international situation that is already rather troubled, I might just point out that this observation about *the general crisis in mass information* has less to do with a problem of the ideological framing of attitudes following the collapse of the communist bloc and more to do with the decisive evolution of computerized weapons systems in a new war, in which the speed of real-time intelligence and monitoring prevails over the former echeloned maneuver of battalions in combat zones.

After all, as that prophet of doom of Soviet power, Admiral Gorchkov, claimed a few years ago: "The winner of the next war will be the side that made the most of the electromagnetic spectrum."

What can we say today of the winner of the post–Cold War, except that madly making the most of the airwaves involves the use of telecommunications and jamming not only in the military realm but also in the civilian. Following censorship and propaganda, the days of *strategic disinformation* and manipulation of opinion are here. Following the "total war" once launched on the seas before being repatriated to land, the age of a "nodal war" has dawned, flickering a year ago in the electromagnetic ether above the Persian Gulf. What are the odds that, for want of a battlefield or some such "theater of operations," the small screen won't tomorrow hold some nasty surprises and more than a few optical illusions in the political field?

Indeed, the Gulf War has marked the beginning of serious doubts about the reign of instant information: Can one democratize ubiquity, instantaneity, immediacy, which are precisely the prerogatives of the divine—in other words, of autocracy?

So many questions posing the problem of the limits of possibility for traditional political practices.

As contemporary societies experience a sort of personality split with regard to time—at least, to the moment—with *the present* of immediate life on one hand and *the telepresent* of mass communication on the other, surely it would be appropriate to pose the problem of the effect of the temporal regime of human perception on our understanding and thus on our capacities for political expression and decision-making.

Surely the pragmatic nature of parliamentary democracy should incite us to consider not only the diversity of opinion but also the individual's psycho-physiological limits when it comes to interpreting the unexpected, what crops up *ex abrupto*.

Asked by journalists in November 1991 whether live television broadcast had any negative effects, French philosopher Marcel Gauchet responded: "It should be the other way around! It's the slowness of information that really opened the way for disinformation. *It's not a question of time but of a state of mind.*"[2]

As though a "state of mind" were not directly influenced by the speed of a message! As though technological progress were neutral when it comes to the autonomy of thought, the authority of the individual! As though conditioning, putting people under their influence, depended merely on the good or bad will of organs of the press . . . Why this obliviousness to the urgency, this negation of the disastrous effects of speed on the interpretation of events?

From ancient Athens up to the transportation revolution of the nineteenth century, the *democratization of relative speed* was a major historical constant in the development of Western civilization. But can we seriously envisage *a similar democratization of absolute speed* in the age of the instantaneous transmission revolution?

Personally I doubt it, for, as Seneca said, "The inert man gets in his own way."[3]

30 January 1992

The Gulf War began with the frenetic clapping and cheering of the crews of the American battleships *Wisconsin* and *Missouri* greeting the launch of the Tomahawk cruise missiles, programmed automata. It ended with that notorious episode in which the soldiers of the routed Iraqi army surrendered to a drone, a reduced-scale remotely piloted vehicle of aerial reconnaissance.

Thus in the Middle East we saw a robotization of war that involved the definitive removal of men of arms from combat, and in the United States the exacerbation of a new will to power, of America's sense of superiority vis-à-vis its own allies and recent enemies.

From time immemorial, Westerners, and Anglo-Saxons in particular, have derived a sense of superiority from their technical superiority, a determination to treat the rest of the world as nothing more than an object predestined for their machinations. This arrogant presumption derives most intimately and, I would say, "clinically," from a power relationship maintained since antiquity with a population of ever more efficient and numerous automata. This deviance means that, when it comes to the crunch, as Merleau-Ponty remarked, "A Cartesian no longer even sees himself in his own mirror; he sees only a dummy, an unreal double."

Five
The Near-Death Experience

A personal relationship with an inhuman double would explain the ecstasy of the crewmen of the *Wisconsin* and the *Missouri* at the takeoff of the Tomahawks, those oh-so-"smart" weapons equipped with inertial guidance systems and terrain-following radar that directed them infallibly to the end of their course, the final explosion more than a thousand kilometers away . . . Like unrepentant fetishists marveling at the remote manipulation of some wax or wooden figurine, a magic rite whose object is to direct an occult force toward a chosen act or the distant destruction of beings and things, thanks to the diversion of their digitalized image or of their radar ghost; the restitution of an old power ritual that comes from who knows where—maybe the age-old origins of an *applied science* that believes it is beyond superstition yet merely returns to it.

The principal characteristic of this scientific fetishism is thus its incantatory aspect, which means that "when a model has been successful in one order of problems, science tries it out everywhere," as Merleau-Ponty further writes. And so Westerners grew used to *seeing androids everywhere*, a bit the way Descartes, in denying the power of sensory knowledge, ended up acquiring a somewhat surrealist view of the world. He wrote: "When looking from a window and saying I see men who pass in the street, I really do not see them, but infer that what I see is men. . . . And yet what do I see from the window but hats and coats which may cover automatic machines? Yet I judge these to be men. And similarly solely by the faculty of judgment which rests in my mind, I comprehend that which I believed I saw with my eyes."[1]

The android attribution, whether involving pure mechanics or some figuration of the living being, thus offers no Promethean vision of the world but the reverse: a nihilistic coming of its image, a tendency to break up the original unity of beings and things by means of those machines and automata, each of which is, in its own way, a scrap of movement, a piece of intellection, an animal portion, a spare part of time . . . This dissection being made official at the end of the Age of Enlightenment when the *trunk of the tree of knowledge* (philosophy–physics and technology–theology) splintered and the French revolutionaries, with their baying cult of the "Goddess Reason," declared a sort of deification of the android model, proffered to the crowds as a *substitute faith*, a new state religion.

If one eliminates God and if, soon after, it becomes fashionable to declare Him dead, it is only normal that, through successive shifts, one ends up getting a little anxious about the origins of this "man" who, once removed from the Judeo-Christian Genesis, suddenly finds himself robbed of his inheritance, deprived of identity. Here again, they will try out the android expedient; they will invent a keyword, *hominoid* (followed by sundry anthropoids, hominids, etc.), to designate a category simultaneously comprising the great apes, said to be "superior" (chimpanzee, gorilla, orangutan), and man, who, according to Michel Foucault, "is only a recent invention, a figure not yet two centuries old, a new wrinkle in our knowledge who will disappear again as soon as that knowledge has discovered a new form."[2] Between the man-machine Descartes saw from his window and the laboratory animal of physiologist Claude Bernard—and thanks to a series of *jeux de mots* and *jeux de sens*—the evolutionary monkey did indeed become a being who, though not yet exactly "man," nonetheless possessed a latent "superior mind" in a body-machine somewhat inferior and homely. And so it would suffice to straighten him up, to set him nicely upright on his hind legs, for his cortex finally to be at ease in his cranial box—as was later asserted by the zealots of a phrenology since forgotten. This mutant would thus reach the summit of the hierarchy of living beings, regaining, to everyone's satisfaction, a place equivalent to the one he had occupied in Genesis; better still, through the infallible mechanisms of applied science, he would *take the place of God*, thus completing the religious parody of the Incarnation. Echoed by the media, such a fantastic event was to captivate the general public—and artists too—for nearly two hundred years.

Born in the same year as Darwin (1809) and a contemporary of Mary Shelley, Edgar Allan Poe was interested in quite a number of automatons, such as Charles Babbage's calculating machine, an ancestor of the computer, before becoming passionately interested in Johann Maelzel's mysterious chess player. Having observed that this player did not win every game, Poe concluded that it had to be a man inside a machine. And so we went from the metempsychosis of the evolutionary monkey to the embodiment of a human mind *in an android;* why not move on after that to those *evolving machines* whose rituals could be jolted into action by their own energy potential, their own creative accidents? The guillotine, capable of reliably providing instant death, fascinated not only the physiologists of the day but also poets such as Villiers de l'Isle-Adam, author of *L'Eve future*, who watched, at the foot of the scaffold, for the exact moment that "life" left the body of the executed.

Another avatar: in the 1968 film *2001, A Space Odyssey*, the *robot-navigator* of the spacecraft formed "human relationships" with certain members of the crew . . . and died as a result!

In *Blade Runner*, in 1982, synthetic creatures known as "replicants" end up nostalgically declaring themselves "in love with life," even though they are not living beings.

Parallel to this constant movement that drives researchers themselves to endow robots with traces of a sentient existence, a new fashion is taking off, particularly in the United States: *that of loving one's death.*

Promoting a sort of *aesthetics of disappearance*, the NDE (Near Death Experience) movement incites its adherents to dream of *leaving their bodies* and, with the aid of a few slugs of endorphins, taking round trips to the border of life and clinical death[3]—to experience, in this brush with the old-fashioned coma, an "Edenic postmortem initiation."

It's impossible not to think again of Foucault. If Western man really is only a fragile figure arising from his language, "a face drawn in sand at the edge of the sea,"[4] he would be the only creature who, knowing this language, could eliminate his own invention, that is, himself . . . as though, over the last few centuries, all man had actually managed to do was play the film of Genesis backward, thus never ceasing to near his end.

28 May 1991

You can see hell much better from a basement window than if you take it all in at once.
—*Jules Barbey d'Aurevilly*

In his work *Die Distanz*, videomaker Marcel Odenbach opens up the possibility of a little-exploited aesthetics, the aesthetics of anorthoscopic vision. This involves restricting vision by masking all but the barest slit of the visual field, so that a figure is not seen all at once but is successively revealed. The search for the minimum that one can perceive thus appears to be a paradoxical objective: how can you see *without* seeing, perceive without knowing what you really perceive? The final question is, how far you can take blindness and still maintain form recognition?

We are well aware that we can see clearly what is in front of us because we cannot see what is behind us *at the same time*. Similarly, we observe the near and the far because we cannot see the inside and the outside of things *together*. The frame, the limit of visibility, is clearly what makes conscious objectification possible. We combine our search to maximize perception at all costs with the quest for minimal perception by means of a *slit*, a slit that limits without ever ruling out our perceiving the whole of the object or image masked . . .

Numerous experiments have sought to analyze scientifically the reasons why such occultation is ineffective, but they have never managed to come to grips with the nature of such *perceptionless* perception. This degree zero of the visible becomes an enigma, not only in terms of the space of the image but especially of the time involved in its immediate perception, the *real* time of contemplation, during which the "actual" image glimpsed through the slit is closely integrated with the "virtual" image of the *delayed* interpretation that completes and supplies what is missing in the form perceived by eye movement, by the "tracking" that is indispensable to contemplation. Listen to a specialist in anorthoscopic optics: "To perceive a figure anorthoscopically, it is not enough to know one is looking through a slit; the slit must be seen. . . . The shape of the aperture has an important influence on what is perceived. . . . One can formulate a general hypothesis that eye movement is a clue to figure motion under anorthoscopic conditions. . . . It is evident that tracking is an important determinant of the anorthoscopic figure percept. We believe the major reason for this is that movement of the eyes provides an effective clue that a figure is moving back and forth behind the slit."[1]

We should point out that such "tracking" is another form of occultation. Shifting your gaze, whether thanks to the mobility of your head or the motility of your eyeball, also means effectively shifting your blindness, your own relative blindness, just as much as moving the slit does.

Standing still in front of the video monitor, Odenbach's viewers are thus lured into a "tracking race" with the fleeting image, forced constantly to accelerate their interpretation of the scenes that successively run past them. As in an eye therapy exercise, they have no choice but to train their gaze in visual economy: to economize on space and, especially, to economize on time, for the delay in appearing on the screen always prevails over the visible surface of the sequences projected.

And so it is a race between the gaze's quick "objective" survey and the "subjective" (or mental) interpretation of the images that are viewed successively through the slit—sixty images per second being the limit of conscious perception allowed by the photogram or videogram, and twenty milliseconds the time required for image recognition.

Odenbach's video game is played between these two speeds of acquisition of objectivity. Beyond that, there is nothing to see.

Die Distanz, the title of the work, is thus the distance that separates not the visible from the invisible but clairvoyance from nonclairvoyance or, more precisely, belief from disbelief.

Since there is most certainly a complicity between *seeing* and *believing,* a complicity desired by the videomaker, the rapidity of shape recognition depends above all on the rapidity of "faith," that *perceptual faith* that once lent its name to the gun's line of sight ("line of faith" in French). We might recommend such a spiritual exercise not only to those who no longer believe in anything but, especially, to those who no longer believe their eyes: *optical atheists,* those baffled beings no longer capable of taking an interest in the shape of a world that is passing faster and faster . . .

"Hesitation is a logical crossroads. If you don't get past the hesitation barrier, you regress toward dogmatism, a kind of rigidity. . . . But if you get over this hump, you find yourself at an anthropological junction, faced with two paths—one, belief, the other, desire—that allow you to gain access to a sort of mutation in existence," psychoanalyst Jean Oury writes in a recent work.[2]

A perceptual hesitation barrier, Odenbach's *slit* is also a sort of *logical crossroads* that forces the viewer to choose. Otherwise he too regresses, refusing all subjective recognition of sequences. *A dumbfounded spectator,* he then retreats, like a "conscientious objector," into his refusal to believe what he sees.

Since *seeing* is also *believing* that you see correctly what you most often notice casually, Odenbach's anorthoscopic work trains us to reject any pathological fixation of the gaze, a fixation that would soon lead to a form of *optical dogmatism,* a rigidity of observation that would rule out the "mutation in existence" of which Oury speaks, a mutation that is only ever the *relativistic commutation* of what passes and what goes past our very eyes, here and now.

This was the formidable situation confronting the nineteenth century's triumphant objectivism, but even more so, perhaps, confronting the boom in a *passive* (geometrical) optics that revealed the reality of a world supposedly "whole"— a *globalizing* and maximizing conception of the real that collapsed at the beginning of the twentieth century, in the face of the progress in relativity and in an *active* (physical) optics which led, conversely, to a fragmentary and minimizing conception of present reality.

Today, research on anorthoscopic vision, like research in fractal geometry, has further bolstered this admission of the bankruptcy of "optical positivism" by concluding that *the whole, the global*, certainly exist, only surely not in the eye of the beholder—in his desire, perhaps, his hopes for the future of images, the ocular kinematics of the immediate.

We come across this problem of the temporality of "active" or "adaptive" optics again in a recent study on the subliminal speeding up of video. The time slot in which the image runs past is always restricted in the same manner as the physical slit, thus proving, as though there were any doubt, not only that all *clairvoyance* is *belief*, but also that optics *is* kinematic, ocular perception being inseparable from the speed of acquisition of scenes perceived.

If speed then serves *to see*, to conceive—that is, to seize reality, and not just to get around—this is because it is part and parcel of perceptual faith, that ocular belief that is inseparable from our immediate awareness. "Belief" or "desire": the choice offered by the forking path of perception is clear; the more readily you accede to the scenes that unfold before you, the more consistency you give your existence. Your existence suddenly becomes *commutative* with an environment to which you lend credence . . . Otherwise, you soon regress to a *dogmatism of appearances* not far removed from autism.

As you can see, the interest of Odenbach's *Die Distanz* is twofold, for it offers its audience on the one hand masked scenes of history representing *total* war, and on the other the freedom to choose to refuse to see them for what they are: the initial cause of the breakdown of a continent, the division of Germany.

An anorthoscopic *slit* for an anachronistic *wall*, an iron curtain that has just now disappeared, been wiped out, because the peoples involved no longer believed in the totalitarian ideology imposed upon them for too long, but in their *freedom to choose* . . . An economic and political mutation once again based on a commutation of interests and desires, a *commutation of existence* between East and West.

27 November 1989

"Painting cannot deceive us, for it does not have at its disposal the real hue of the light," wrote Schlegel in the nineteenth century.

What can we say today about the deceit of the *live* television image except that it does possess that "real hue," thanks to the speed of light of physical optics? That real hue is nothing other than the real time of television broadcasts, which sheds light on the reality of the scenes observed. Whereas pictorial representation could not pretend to compensate for immediate lighting—all shapes formerly being registered in *delayed time*—thanks to the technologies of live broadcasting, television presentation does possess that light of immediacy, that sudden *credibility* that neither painting nor photography nor even cinema ever had . . . Whence the emergence of a last *horizon of visibility*, from the moment you reduce the optical thickness of the human environment.

Currently, if the televised event does in fact take *place*, it nonetheless enlightens us about its ultimate limit, that of the *absolute* speed of light.

Seven
Light Time

From now on, man makes use not only of the *relative* speed of the animal or the machine, but also of the speed of electromagnetic wave trains, without realizing that here he comes up against an insuperable barrier; no longer the sound or heat barriers that are commonly broken by supersonic or hypersonic vehicles, but the barrier of light, the ultimate boundary of an energy intensity that forever limits human action and perception.

Indeed, as we too often forget, if the event does in fact take place *here and now*, it equally takes place *in the light* of a positive or a negative acceleration. For example, the fortuitous sidewalk encounter of two pedestrians who hail one another is not of the same nature as the unexpected encounter of two motorists driving slowly past each other down the road and waving to each other as they go by this same sidewalk.

Imagine for a moment that the two vehicles about to pass each other here and now were sped up considerably; the encounter, the exchange of greetings, would simply not take place unless there was sufficient time for perception, the relative invisibility of the two motorists present having nothing to do with some ghostly absence of their bodies, but solely with the lack of duration required for their mutual apprehension. The event of the pedestrians encountering each other on the sidewalk or of the motorists driving past each other on the road do both take place here and now; but they equally take place *by light*, or, as we often say, *at speed*—a speed relative to the motion of the various mobile bodies.

If, *a contrario*, the two interlocutors communicate with each other through (real-time) interactive technologies, it is the absolute speed of radiation that will facilitate their tête-à-tête, their face-to-face encounter, and this happens no matter what intervals of space and time effectively separate them.

Here, the event *does not take place*, or, more precisely, *it takes place twice*, the topical aspect yielding to the teletopical aspect, the unity of time and place being split between the emission and reception of signals, here and there *at the same time*, thanks to the power of electromagnetic interactivity.

The problem of the *televisual horizon* of the ephemeral encounter, however, remains unresolved: indeed, if the transappearance of the appearance of co-present interlocutors is comparable, if not analogous, to that of the pedestrians or motorists evoked above, the *terminus* of their mutual perception differs. The horizon of the pedestrians who run into each other is the *end of the street;* the horizon of the motorists who pass each other going slowly is the *perspective of the avenue*—the vanishing point of the urban horizon demarcating the area of their effective encounter.

In the case of televiewers co-present in front of their screens, the horizon is not *the background of the image*, but its delimitation: the frame of the screen, the framing of the broadcast, and, especially, the duration accorded to the interview before the cathode screen once again becomes silent and opaque.

The *televisual horizon* is thus uniquely that of the *present* of the real-time emission and reception of the televised interview, *a present instant* precisely defined by the framing of the two televiewers' viewpoints and, especially, by the time limit placed on their face-to-face dialogue.

"To define the present in isolation is to kill it," Paul Klee once wrote. Isn't this the crime that the technologies of telecommunications commit in isolating the *present* from its "here and now," and promoting a *commutative elsewhere* that is no longer the location of our concrete presence in the world, but merely that of a discrete and intermittent telepresence?

The real time of telecommunications is thus opposed not just to the past, to delayed time, but to the present, to its very actuality; an optical switching of the "real" and the "figurative" that refers back to the observer physically present here and now, sole persistence of an illusion in which the body of the witness becomes the unique element of stability in a virtualized environment.

And so the *focusing* of the gaze of the film viewer, eyewitness to the *small-scale optical illusion* resulting from retinal persistence alone, is superseded by this *polarization* of the body of the televiewer, witness to the *large-scale electro-optical illusion* that turns the reality of the whole world into a production—the on-the-spot persistence of the witness's body completing the persistence of his ocular system. *Inertia of one's own body,* apparent result of this general influx of (optical and sound) information whereby everything converges and concentrates on the being attentive to the *no-delay path* of images and sounds, the screen suddenly becoming a last "visible horizon," a horizon of accelerated particles that takes over from the geographic horizon of the expanse in which the televiewer's body still moves.

Apparent horizon or deep horizon? The question of the optical thickness of the real environment arises again today for the inhabitant of this constricted planet, the question of the direct and customary transparency of materials—with the addition of the enigma of this indirect transappearance that derives from the capabilities of the "active" optics of the *indirect light* that illuminates the human habitat, just as the *direct light* of the sun or the electricity fairy once lit and revealed our surroundings, thanks to the properties of the "passive" optics of the various corrective materials such as air, water, or the glass in our lenses!

We all know *there is no apparent speed without a horizon, a terminus.* Has the frame of the cathode screen become for us a real horizon, *a square horizon?* This square which is no more than a cube hiding within the two dimensions of the reductive and fragmentary image of the televised sequence? The question remains.

As you will note, the irruption at this end of the millennium of an *indirect horizon,* fruit of the appearance of a "third interval" of the *light* type (neutral sign), alongside the traditional intervals of *space* (negative sign) and *time* (positive sign), leads to the unexpected invention of one final *perspective* in which the depth of real time wins out over the depth of the real space of territories. At this point, the indirect light of signals illuminates the world of sense experience *a giorno* by momentarily reducing the *optical thickness* of our planet to nothing.

To the spatio-temporal distortions of distance and the delays due to the very rapidity of transport, of the physical displacement of people, is now added the fluctuation of these appearances instantaneously transmitted at a distance . . . Interactive technologies that favor an as yet unperceived event, this *sudden cybernation of geophysical space and its atmospheric volume*—and not merely of the machine or object, as occurred with the invention of the first automatons. This time it means the establishment of a kind of control of the geophysical environment whereby the visual piloting that is the instantaneous coming together of places would supersede the piloting of vehicles that still move around in those places . . . A telescoping of the near and the far, the world's expanse suddenly becoming thin, "infra-thin," thanks to the capacity for *optical magnification* of the appearances of the human environment.

"*The authentic observer is truly an artist:* he divines what is significant and is good at sniffing out and retaining what matters in the fleeting and peculiar mix of phenomena," wrote the German poet Novalis.

You'd be hard-pressed to find a better description of the energy of observation—image energy or, more precisely, *information energy.*

Indeed, if speed is not strictly speaking a phenomenon but the relationship *between* phenomena (relativity itself), and if speed allows us to see and to conceive and not just to get around more easily, Novalis has described absolutely accurately the *kinematic optics* of that gaze that strives to retain the essential in the ephemeral movement of phenomena. Incidentally, this is what computer scientists today call *image capacity.*

Along the lines of the microprocessors of computer-generated imagery, the human eye is a powerful instrument for analyzing the structures of the visible, one capable of quickly grasping the optical depth of events (twenty milliseconds); so much so that it seems necessary today to add to the two usual types of energy—*potential* (latent) energy and *kinetic* (active) energy—a third and final type: *kinematic* (information) energy. Without this, it would seem, the relativistic nature of our ability to observe would disappear, once again disconnecting the observer and the observed, which is how things were in the past, in the age before Galileo.

But let us abandon this futile historical regression and return to the technologies of real time.

Having succeeded in broadcasting at the limit speed of elementary particles electro-optical images and electro-acoustic sounds, as well as telemetric signals that enable not only teleaudition or television but also teleaction, laboratories supported by their respective governments are now tackling improvements in the resolution of the televised image, in order to speed up this indirect transparency and further enhance the optical magnification of the natural environment.

Remember that the human gaze *carves up* both space and time at once, the eye's objectivity thus bringing off a relativistic feat, the limits of the visual field and the succession of sequences further combining with the temporal carving up of the rhythmics of the image. *The act of the discriminating gaze* is thus not a hollow notion; if it were, the relativity of the visible would itself be merely a hallucination of perspective!

The quest for high-definition television (HDTV) along with the quest for high-fidelity teleaudition thus participate in the scientific controversy over "observed energy." In fact, once contemporary physicists have convinced us that the observer is inseparable from the thing observed, one may legitimately wonder what has happened to the objective credibility of this observed energy that is the basis of all measurement in the realm of the experimental sciences . . .

Observed energy or observation energy? The question remains, though this does not prevent us from achieving, through research on high definition, a live televised image whose imperfections are imperceptible to the naked eye, the resolution of the electronic image now surpassing that of our eyesight—and this *to the point where the image is made more real than the thing of which it is merely, precisely, an "image"!* A stupefying phenomenon, made possible, for one thing, by acceleration from twenty-five to fifty images per second, the subliminal limit of human perception being, as you will recall, sixty images a second.

And so, the *optical magnification* of our natural environment is emerging at this fin de siècle as the final "frontier," the last horizon of technological activity. Improving the precision of telereal observation is today's analogue to the conquest of territories or the expansion of empires, the recently popularized term *glasnost* being in no way innocent!

Just after the events that took place in Eastern Europe, a representative from a neighboring EEC country said: "If you get rid of borders, you must also get rid of distances, otherwise we'll have big problems in the outlying areas." In my view, this phrase should be turned around to make sense of the political stakes of the moment. If you get rid of distances, in fact, and this has already happened with the recent development of telecommunications, you must also get rid of borders. Not just the political borders of nation-states, in favor of federal or confederative entities; you must also abolish the *aesthetic* "borders" of the things that surround us, in favor of one ultimate boundary in time, that of the acceleration of the *optical commutation* of the appearances of a world wholly telepresent, twenty-four hours a day, seven days a week.

Speeding up the still-intermittent thinning of the optical layer that is the visible horizon of a planet overexposed to the technologies of interactivity, just as the time distances of physical travel have been growing shorter ever since the transportation revolution, means further increasing the intensity of the lighting provided by this second sun that illuminates the expanse of our territories the way meteorological satellites reveal their climates . . .

The end of the outside world, of this *mundus* of immediate appearances that still necessitated physically moving about, negotiating an interval of space and a certain span of time; "negative" and "positive" intervals singularly devalued by the interval of the absolute speed of light, the "neutral" interval of those waves responsible for the television broadcast that challenges not only the philosophical notion of *present time* but, especially, the notion of the *real instant.*

For some of us, the risk, the proximity of death gives each moment of our lives more intensity, more depth. Surely we can tell, *a contrario,* that in giving more *depth* to the present "instant," these new electromagnetic technologies will ruin us and literally kill us; television's so-called *real* instant only ever being that of the sudden disappearance of our *immediate consciousness.* The present instant can be endlessly intensified only to the detriment of that "intuition of the moment" dear to Gaston Bachelard. With the teletechnologies of the video signal, it is no longer a question of some "petty illusion" like the one that frightened those watching the Lumière brothers' film *L'Entrée du train en gare de La Ciotat* in 1895. It is a question of a liberating "grand illusion," that of the presence right here of the far corners of the globe. A telepresence as little reassuring as that of the locomotive plunging into the audience of the first film screenings.

While the relative speed of the shots comprising the photogram merely brought about *the apparent movement* of the Lumière brothers' film, the absolute speed of the videogram reveals *the apparent proximity of the antipodes,* reaching the limit of visibility, since the purely mechanical unwinding of sequences at seventeen or twenty-four images a second is now superseded by that of the electronic frame of the video image at twenty-five, thirty, or fifty images a second.

Killing the immediate present, then, is only possible on the express condition of also killing the televiewer's *mobility in space*, for the questionable benefit of a pure and simple *on-the-spot motility*; isolating the "present" consisting especially in isolating the "patient," isolating him once and for all from the active world of sensory experience of the space that surrounds him, and instead promoting simple *image feedback*—in other words, a return to the inertia of one's own body, to this supposedly interactive hand-to-hand combat.

By way of conclusion, we might note that the "global village" Marshall McLuhan hoped for does not exist; there is only *a center of inertia* that freezes the present world within each of its inhabitants. A return to the zero point of some originary populating process, one no longer so much concerned with the earth's expanse, the urbanization of the real space of our planet, as with the *urbanization of the real time* of its mere appearances and of the intermittent eclipse of the speaking beings that we are.

31 March 1990

When it comes to information, be especially wary of
plausibility. Always begin by believing the unbelievable.
—Emile Gaboriau

The innovation of the ship already entailed the innovation
of the shipwreck. The invention of the steam engine, the locomotive, also entailed the invention of derailment, the rail
disaster. The same goes for nascent aviation, airplanes inno-
vating the crash on the ground, the air disaster. To say nothing of the automobile and the pile-up at high speed, or of
electricity and electrocution, or especially of those major
technological hazards resulting from the development of
the chemical and nuclear industries. Each period of
technical evolution, with its set of instruments and machines, involves the appearance of specific accidents,
revealing in negative the growth of scientific
thought.

Since the military object—armaments or
sundry projectiles—reverses this tendency to
privilege the *substance*, the genius of war demands, *a contrario*, the primary invention
of the *accident*, the disaster. The gun, cannon, tank, and missile are in the end
merely cumbersome *military hardware*
which it makes sense to lighten and miniaturize while their destructive power (impact, range) is endlessly increased, made
more spectacular, with the ultimate aim of inventing the *absolute weapon* (atomic or other), an
absolute form of major technological hazard, of
fear, and hopefully of the beginning of wisdom.
Actually the beginning of wisdom would above
all mean recognizing the symmetry between substance and accident, instead of constantly trying to hide
it. Acquiring a tool, any new piece of equipment, indus-

Eight
The Accident Museum

trial or otherwise, means also acquiring a particular danger; it means opening your door and exposing your private world to minor or major hazards.

To censor this self-evident observation, which is, alas, what happens, is *to practice dissimulation*, meaning disinformation, thereby contributing to a loss of confidence in the efficacy of science analogous to the loss of confidence now affecting politics. Whence this disaffection, this decline in curiosity in the most various areas, given the unprecedented development of electronic and other imagery—though the *simulation industry* has recently provided an exception and, indeed, even a certain compensation.

To expose the accident so as no longer to expose oneself to the accident is now, in fact, the principal function of simulators used to drive technological engines. It seems to me that the same principle should apply to the new museography, in particular to the museography that claims to deal with the sciences and the products of industry.

Now that a new French science museum is opening at La Villette, it is time to unmask industry's other face, too long hidden, whose features are failure and breakdown. Not to achieve some "anti-science museum,"[1] but to try to demonstrate what the very notion of "museum" might mean as applied to practices deriving from experimental research—thus helping to establish what may well one day be *the science of the anti-museum*, a public platform for what never gets exposed, but exposes us endlessly to major hazards.

At a time when the lead stories in the newspapers and on television news are almost always about voluntary or involuntary accidents, tragedies, and natural or terrorist-induced catastrophes, the problem for scientific museology is not so much one of choosing between a gallery of machines, a *garbage dump museum* of the Arts et Métiers kind, or some kind of *laboratory museum* like the Palais de la Découverte. The problem is one of "positivism" in science and philosophy; of the publicist's lyrical illusion of a kind of "progress" that endlessly erases and conceals its negative implications *in the very name of science!* . . . As though research in the exact sciences could progress by dissimulation, by censoring mistakes and miscalculations.

It is urgent that we finally make room in the realm of public information for *fallibilism*, the tendency among certain theoreticians to promote research into refutation within the field of each scientific discipline. This approach is postpositivist to the extent that it finally agrees to go beyond an ideology of progress, linear and uninterrupted, excluding the importance of the mishap or the beneficial mistake.

Note that this is not a matter of redeeming the traditional criticism or self-criticism of researchers but of *reversing the relationship to proof:* proof through failure, exemplary refutation, and no longer exclusively through spectacular success.

For our anti-museum of accident simulation—unlike the all too common museum of substance dissimulation, where display is used to cover up the truth—it would be a matter of *reversing the relationship to exposure, to exhibition,* as with experimental methods of approximation whereby, unable to attain the object, you keep testing to determine *what it cannot be.*

Or perhaps it is like professional simulation processes that accumulate negative situations: not to terrorize the experimenters (drivers, engineers) but to accustom them to the *unusual,* preparing them to react in a predictable and effective way and to avoid the dangers of habit, the professional distortion that comes from taking the reliability of technology for granted.

To expose, to exhibit the accident is thus *to expose the unlikely, to expose the unusual and yet inevitable.*

Infallibility just does not exist in the areas under consideration. The major accident of the space shuttle *Challenger* is there to prove it yet again. Besides, if we look at what happened there with such recent technology (four or five years old at most), we see clearly that NASA's arrogance in playing down the risks was to blame. With a launch process as disparate as NASA's, which simultaneously hooks up the space shuttle (sophisticated), the two boosters (solid-state booster rockets not much different from the V-2s of the last world war), and the enormous cylinder of liquid hydrogen, *the accident was not so much that the shuttle exploded in flight but that it managed to get off the ground!*

All "limit situations" require vigilance against habituation, and the same should apply to the realm of information about "limit technologies"—as much for the sake of the professionals in charge of the programs and other performers and decision makers as for amateurs, the naive audience for the technological feats of the moment.

In this sense, exhibiting the sciences and technologies of the fin de siècle bears little relation to the display cases on show at the museum of La Villette. But it bears a close relation to the *Challenger* explosion above the Kennedy Space Center live before several million viewers installed in front of their cathode display cases.

To expose or be exposed, that is the question. To be or not to be aware, scientifically speaking, of the danger of the unexpected: the accident, the hidden side of any natural or man-made substance. As all studies of simulation now privilege research into surprise, the expecting of the unexpected, Aristotle's phrase "There is no science of the accident" should be immediately rejected, for the new generation of image simulators constitutes just such a "science," gradually unmasking the accidental. This was once almost impossible to imagine, the options for scientific exposure and speculation being too narrowly restricted (like those of art) to *the sphere of human accessibility.* In other words, to our capacity to perceive the environment, a capacity tied exclusively to our organs of perception. Today those organs are wired to an impressive array of (audiovisual or automobile) prostheses that enable us to *indirectly* access another space-time in order to grasp limit phenomena.

"What happens is so far ahead of our thinking or our intentions that we can never catch up with it and never know its true appearance," Rainer Maria Rilke once wrote.

This acknowledgment of our shortcomings, even if it retains its profound truth, no longer completely fits the current situation, since the objective of most *digital display* is precisely to update this out-of-date appearance, this surprise constituted by rupture, sudden dysfunctioning, or serious parasitic noise.

How can they then have the nerve to present the feats of rationality to the public in a place that was, let's not forget, the theater of a monumental programming error, without first exhibiting that other feat of science constituted by the meteorological forecasting of catastrophes? *The exploration of time to come*, this "weather" that is the space of tomorrow, the speed-space of what crops up out of the blue—for machines, for people, for society itself—through the economic and political fallout of resounding failures.

At a time when the public is interested in the meteoric feats of Halley's comet, it would perhaps be appropriate to mentally picture each incident, each accident that occurs, as a sort of "factual meteorite" whose impact is prepared in the dark, within the time depth of materials, of the machine; a propitious darkness, analogous to that of a firmament concealing future collisions.

From this preventive angle, the accident is no longer to be identified solely with its disastrous consequences, its practical results—ruins and scattered debris—but with a dynamic and energetic process, *a kinetic and kinematic sequence* that has nothing to do with the vestiges of objects destroyed, with wreckage and rubble.[2]

And so exhibiting the accident, *exposing what usually exposes us*, would require a new museography, a sort of "meta-museography" of the overexposure and underexposure of matter and systems at risk, a way of *showing what happens in what crops up out of the blue*, in which blitz cinemacrophotography, video, and computer graphics would be absolutely essential.

Clearly, it would no longer be a matter of exposing new objects, reliefs of various accidents, to the morbid curiosity of visitors in order to achieve some new romanticism of the technological ruin, like a derelict who embellishes his wounds to soften up the passerby. Having polished the brass of the first steam trains in the museums of the twentieth century, we are hardly going to deliberately blacken the charred remains of state-of-the-art technologies! No, it would be a matter of creating a new kind of scenography in which *only what explodes and decomposes is exposed.* A paradoxical mise-en-scène of the obscene in which decomposition and disintegration would finally supersede the compositions of advertising and high-tech "design."

An "aesthetics of disappearance," whether gradual or instantaneous; no longer an aesthetics of appearance, of the progressive emergence of a style, genre, or scientific author. Visitors would no longer file along galleries, past picture rails, since the exhibition space would itself have lost its interest, its museographic appeal, in favor of an *exposure time*, of a time depth comparable to that of the widest horizons, the most immense landscapes: a *landscape of events* that would thus replace the former exhibition hall, an architectural space disqualified on the one hand by its orthogonal geometry[3] and on the other by the requirements of an urgent screening of the phases of the accident. A public screening that clearly has nothing in common with any "hanging" of graphic or photographic works, any kind of exhibition of industrial objects or projects. In the end, as we have just seen this Tuesday, 18 February, on the one o'clock TV newscast, with the live demolition of the frame of the Debussy building at La Courneuve—an eight-second transmutation of a public housing block one hundred and eighty meters high into seventy thousand tons of rubble—the *accident museum* exists. I've come across it: it is a TV screen.

20 February 1986

The year of signs, 1986, is coming to an end, a year full of major accidents: signs in the heavens, the apocalypse of the American space shuttle . . . a sign in the clouds of radioactive Europe . . . a sign in the waters of the Rhine . . . a sign of all our domestic fears, quakes of earth, sea, and air, of our nerves badly strained by the little televised terrors of a war at home, by everyday terrorism in Paris, London, Berlin . . .

Relieved to be done with it, we will celebrate less the New Year than the vanishing of the year gone by, only too happy to forget it. Besides, isn't this fête, this reverse bliss, characteristic of our era, of our times? The era of an overeagerness in our activities, public and private, that pushes us *to desire lack* or absence more than presence, asceticism more than gratification, gain, the abundance of goods. Maybe that is what the feast of Christmas is—no longer a license for the rampant consumption that fills restaurants and auditoriums so much as a "peace of nerves for the sick at heart" that Henri Michaux once yearned for. Sensory deprivation, the pleasure of disillusionment with material progress, pushing us to get back to the source of our expectation and our attention to what amounts to nothing, or nearly nothing.

No longer to travel, except on the spot. No longer to stretch ourselves, to spread ourselves thin in the passing distraction of a physical journey, but just to relax here and now, in the inertia of immobility regained. *Social quietism* leads our societies to wrap themselves in the shroud of interior comfort, the bliss of a reverse vitality in which lack of action becomes the height of passion. A society of hardened lounge lizards, where everyone hopes not to

Nine
Peace of Nerves

die or suffer, as Western masochism has been said to want, but *to be dead.*

The whole panoply of the latest technologies invites us suddenly to be stuck at home, under the house arrest of telematics and the electronic workplace, which turn erstwhile televiewers into teleactors in an instantaneous interactivity that exiles us from real space, from contact with our fellow man.

A remarkable convergence between the hidden desire for sensory privatization and this technological assistance, this assisted conception of existence: the pleasure of the rendezvous at a distance, of a get-together without getting together, pleasure without risk of contamination offered by the anonymous telecommunications of the erotic Minitel or the Walkman; abandoning our fellow man in favor of unknown and distant beings who remain aloof, ghosts of no importance who won't mess up our plans.

How can we fail to see behind this the decline in the neighborhood unit, in the attraction of one's quarter, one's neighbors, in favor of exotic regions and spaces? How can we fail to recognize the defeat of the nuclear family, to the dubious advantage of the *part-time couple,* the single-parent family of the divorced, atomic disintegration of the demographic unit, imminent advent of a bionic Christmas, of a purely scientific nativity? New Year's festivities? No, the dawn of the age of lack, of compulsory asceticism for unproductive, immobilized beings—as everything, good or bad, now comes to us without our having to budge.

In the age of stress, this traumatism of the end of time, season's greetings might go something like this: "Don't send me any more Christmas cards, don't invite me out too often. Phone me, that will do just fine, since my answering machine will pick up for me."

"Leave me alone for a few more days. Whatever you do, don't come to the door, I'm not home for anyone."

"Stop putting your calling card in my mailbox, it's already too full of bills and brochures for me to go near it."

"As for news of the presumed state of the world, my dearest wish is simply for no bombs to go off in department stores or holiday party venues. For none of the usual damage wrought by progress, no more natural or industrial catastrophes, for a world, *my little world*, that's picture-perfect, as untroubled as a Christmas card."

Christmas, a day of rest for our fellows with their bad cases of nerves, peace on earth for our computer-assisted brothers, those spineless creatures, *handicapped voyeurs*, home viewers and operators whose sole vehicle is the armchair in the living room, *spastics* with prosthetic devices for plying the route from home to office, for getting to the getaway at the end of the week, the end of the year, whose flight into Egypt is organized by the transport services, in expectation of the usual massacre of the innocents, the carnage on the roads . . .

Bliss? That might well be "a place where nothing ever happens," where everything remains the same, where there are no further demands on our will and our rare wishes are miraculously granted. Starting with this wish for the absence of all presence. A desire for an anachronistic desert island in these times of numberless crowds, of incommensurable urban concentrations . . .

Asked what was, in his opinion, the greatest modern calamity, an old peasant from the Île-de-France answered without hesitation: "the news." When pressed to explain, he said: "You see, for me the war of 1914 broke out just like that; from one day to the next *we didn't see it coming.* The day before general mobilization, we were calm, no one around here even dreamed there'd be a war and yet we're less than a hundred kilometers from Paris . . . Whereas with radio and now with television, we feel like we're always on the brink of war or some catastrophe, and we can't take it anymore."

The peace of Christmas would probably mean no longer being informed all the time—that is, wildly disinformed about our own current events, those microevents of daily life that ought to shape our judgment, our sense of reality, and that we too often neglect in favor of economic and political events. A fatal interaction between this lack of reality regarding our own intimate lives and the exaggerated presence *in real time* of televised news.

What will happen when we are all hooked up by cable, shackled to the local networks, saturated with satellite news, with commercials, news flashes, intense video clips? The telemanipulation of our opinions, our schedules, risks becoming an electronic torture, an interrogation worthy of the Inquisition.

What will we look forward to when we no longer need to look forward in order to arrive? When we ourselves will have become the films, the programs broadcast into the homes of our distant interlocutors, thanks to the teleconference and the videophone? Probably these questions won't ever be asked, either by the interested parties or by the different authorities involved—governments, trade unions, employers. Cathode ray democracy is an *in vitro* democracy that never entails elections or referenda (with the exception of TV quiz shows), popularity polls measuring audience response only from within the media system.

Wherever the "real time" of instantaneous transmission takes precedence over the real space of a country actually traveled, wherever, as a consequence, the image takes precedence over the thing and the being physically present, there is no longer room for the "public holidays" of a calendar based essentially on night following day. The *electronic day* of telecommunications is no longer the astronomical day of the ephemerides: the indirect lighting of electronic images now replaces electric lighting, just as the latter once replaced sunrise.

Are we not seeing our "cities of light" illuminated less by their neon lights and street lamps than by cameras installed in public places, at intersections, along main roads?

With the laying of fiber-optic cables in Paris, Japan, and elsewhere, the automatic camera and its monitor are supplanting the electrification of town and countryside at the turn of the last century . . . To see, we are no longer content just to dispel darkness, we must also dispel distance through the implacable perspicacity of instant-imaging equipment.

The star of Holy Night, the lights on the Christmas trees, the illumination of display windows and shops, have recently been overtaken by these indiscreet city lights, this *cathode ray window* of a video control room that sometimes makes us into the gifts.

3 December 1986

On Friday, 30 August 1985, at ten o'clock at night in the Place des Innocents near the Forum des Halles, Paris, after a drug dealer is questioned by police, suddenly there is a riot. Close to three hundred people come to the dealer's aid, attacking the police and smashing shop windows. It takes nearly an hour to reestablish calm.

On Monday, 2 September, at the Marseilles housing project La Paternelle, a similar situation is sparked by the killing of a gang member. Following armed robbery and a car chase that ends in a shootout between the robbers and the police, kids from the project side with the gang and harass the state security police who have been called in as reinforcements. The area has to be sealed off for the entire night.

The following Monday, 9 September, in Birmingham, there is a night of rioting in Handsworth after a motorist is ticketed for a traffic violation. In Lozells Road dozens of shops are devastated, a church destroyed, a post office burned down, three people killed and about thirty injured. "Worse than Brixton in 1981!" certain witnesses claim.

Ten
The Fire Tomorrow

One thing these events, distant in space but so very close in time, have in common is their characteristic suddenness, their unpredictability as outbreaks of violence, as well as the flimsiness of the apparent causes; a flimsiness that will lead initial analysts, as usual, to look for deeper, more conventional causes, sociologically speaking, such as unemployment, racism, drugs . . . and to refuse to pay any attention or give credence to the suddenness, the extreme swiftness of the felonies committed, or the temporal convergence of these summer acts of violence, even though certain Jamaican rioters declared: "Soweto, Handsworth, it's all the same struggle!"

What is the analogy here? Can one compare Paris to Marseilles, Marseilles to Birmingham? Or again, this last city to Soweto? Can one in all decency associate South Africa's apartheid with the way immigrants are treated in Britain's industrial agglomerations? Surely not. Despite unemployment and the gravity of the economic crisis, there is no question of race being central. The analogy lies elsewhere, probably in the impact of events in South Africa, a televisual impact that turns Birmingham into a suburb of Soweto. Indeed, this proximity in time explains, better than any well-meaning argument, the quasi-simultaneity of the summer's events.

After more than two months of witnessing live the necessary revolt of the ghettos and the homelands, after sharing week after week in the funerals of the victims of Botha's police, immigrants feel an identification as immediate as the broadcast of the facts, no matter what their race or the conditions of their existence.

The suddenness of the acts of violence in Lozells Road thus has nothing to do with their apparent causes; it results in particular from the extreme state of tension among the most receptive local groups—the idle young or kids on school vacation—who find their true motivation in what is happening thousands of kilometers away during this summer of '85.

The economic decline of Great Britain, by making daily life less appealing for immigrants, shifts their interest to the beyond, the elsewhere. Since in Handsworth, as in Toxteth or Brixton, there is no foreseeable future, *elsewhere begins here*, Soweto is here! Whence the sudden and unpredictable wave of social violence.

Is it really a matter of revolt, of changing the life, the city of Birmingham? Not really, since it is less a matter of solidarity with one's peers, one's immediate neighbors, than of being associated *vicariously through television* with the revolt in the South African antipodes.

As long as we fail to grasp this long-distance interference, this media instantaneity independent of geographic distance, we cannot understand contemporary urban events.

Alongside the territorial town, in fact, there now exists a media nebula whose reality goes well beyond the frontiers of the ghettos, the limits of metropolitan agglomerations. The megalopolis is not Mexico City or Cairo or Calcutta, with their tens of millions of inhabitants, but this sudden temporal convergence that unites actors and televiewers from the remotest regions, the most disparate nations, the moment a significant event occurs here or there.

If the earlier town, with its well-defined and legible land registry, could be administered in a relatively predictable way, the latest city has no chance of being so; it belongs wholly to the age of the random development and thus escapes what was hitherto known as "territorial administration." All the clamoring for local autonomy or independence signals this precarious situation, which good old *decentralization* still claims to have under control.

As far back as August 1965, the riots in Watts gave the signal for the volatile American summers to come, with their processions of ritual destruction and systematic looting, their fires lit to the cry of "Burn, baby, burn!"

Between 1965 and 1967, we were to witness the epidemic constitution of a new entity that spread beyond the confines of the black ghettos of Detroit, Chicago, or Newark. This "social representation," on a true scale with the tragedy of ghettoization, was soon to spread beyond the black population to the university campuses of America and then Europe.

Let us not forget Montreal's days of lawlessness in October 1969, either, with the police arresting other police; or exactly a year later, in October 1970, Quebec's declaration of a state of civil war, with the army occupying the great Canadian metropolis and the unions demanding an end to police terrorism. And remember the demonstrations in Mexico during the same period and their cruel suppression, with close to two hundred dead.

No, clearly, with Birmingham there is no need to refer back to London or Liverpool four years earlier. England does not have a monopoly on urban riots any more than the United States did earlier, as the French and Europeans generally would do well to remember. What happened this summer in Soweto, in Birmingham, Marseilles, or Paris is a warning. Now that the French publisher Stock is bringing out the translation of James Baldwin's latest book, *Murders in Atlanta*, it might be appropriate to read his premonitory essay, published in 1962: "The Fire Next Time."

Much better attuned than most sociologists in vogue at the time, the black novelist foresaw the epidemic of fire, signaling that the fate of "the so-called American Negro" would soon be the fate of all and sundry, no matter what the color of their skin: "The Negro situation is dangerous in a different way, both for the Negro qua Negro and for the country of which he forms so troubled and troubling a part. The American Negro is a unique creation; he has no counterpart anywhere and no predecessors."[1]

With those words Baldwin points up the powerlessness not only of the North American city to integrate its blacks, but of any city to integrate anyone at all from now on. This is a radical inversion of the principle of the traditional town, once a place for integration, for assimilation of communities, of exotic peoples. Today, with the worldwide megalopolis, the town has become a place of accelerated social disintegration, of generalized ghettoization, a precarious juxtaposition of solitary individuals, of diffuse groups that are notoriously unstable: inner cities in Britain, transit camps in France, homelands in South Africa—so far ahead of their time that the most extremist of Afrikaners want the creation not only of independent *black homelands* but also of independent *white homelands*, all floating around like so many croutons in the cultural soup of the South African "nation"!

It is painful, twenty years later, to reread an article by Michel Tatu from *Le Monde* of 3 November 1965, discussing the future of Watts: "Housing could no doubt be materially improved, but it's hard to see how it will be possible to prevent the whites from fleeing their neighborhoods en masse once the blacks begin moving there. The latter will continue to feel left to their own devices, especially in the sprawling city of Los Angeles which has no center or even crowds to blend in with, and where whites only glimpse their fellow human beings through the windshields of their cars. . . . When the Reverend Martin Luther King, speaking in Watts a few days later, called on his colored brothers to 'give each other your hand,' someone in the crowd shouted: 'To burn?'"

This disqualification of an urban space once charged with meaning, built to achieve a greater proximity, the physical contact of the greatest number, began with the industrial revolution, so it is highly symbolic to find Birmingham or Liverpool today, once more, on the front page of the newspapers.

This urban *deregulation* has effectively anticipated that of the new technologies: aeronautics, electronics, computers. Thanks to good old postindustrial restructuring, that sprawling urban wasteland where "users" have contact only through the windshields of their cars is giving way at this very moment to the infinite suburb of an audiovisual no-man's-land peopled by ghosts, by electronic specters that hardly have any contact at all anymore except through the intermediary of a television screen or computer terminal, with their attendant voyeurism and all-out swapping—of sexual partners, shopping tips, sports scores, or purely denunciatory police intelligence. *Audiovisual gropes* for which the annual information technology trade fair does the publicity, perfectly reflecting a communications society that no longer communicates anything but *messages:* data packets addressed to uncertain recipients—a data transfer accident that brings downtowns to the downfall James Baldwin decried some time ago.

18 September 1985

A blood-red headband round his forehead, the man looms up out of the depths of the primal forest, with his bow, his quiver, and his arrows: Geronimo? No, Rambo.

What return of the repressed are we dealing with here? Has the Indian of *Red Power* finally conquered the North American administration? Has the evolution of the Western, already considerable over the last decade or so, with its more and more sympathetic redskins, culminated in the vengeful figure of this hero who rebels against all law, all war? An *outlaw* for whom the adversary is no longer the cavalry but a flotilla of Soviet helicopters launched in his pursuit, just like General Custer's forces in their raids against rebellious Indian tribes. One thing remains constant, though: the camps are still there, but instead of Indian reservations, full of victims of the punitive expeditions of Union soldiers, as in *Little Big Man*, they are gulags, Vietnamese reservations where, they say, some hundreds of prisoners are detained, survivors of the American expeditionary corps.

To speak of fascism in relation to this propaganda-fiction film seems totally ludicrous. You would think our young intellectual critics had forgotten what Italian fascism and Hitler's Nazism were like. Fascism was supposed to be "futurist," while Rambo is resolutely backward-looking. Rambo goes back to hell, to the hell of the prerational origins of war, a war that, far from dragging in the masses, saw the individualism of the warrior triumph over all. It is ultimately in this eternal return of the solitary killer that we should look for the meaning of this blockbuster, in the very extent to which this work is a clinical symptom of the recent evolution of conflict, but also of crime.

Eleven
Mass Murderer

On the one hand, Star Wars, President Reagan's famous Strategic Defense Initiative, on the other, Rambo, this hero with such a sweet smile who is now featured in U.S. Army recruitment posters.

Note too that Sylvester Stallone's film ends with the symbolic destruction of military high-tech by our Reaganite hero, as though there were a contradiction, a secret opposition, between the mission of Rambo-Geronimo and the equally Reaganite project of Star Wars. Opposition or unavowed complementarity between state terrorism and the grandiose antimissile defense project of the United States.

Let's go over the course of the military history of the last forty years: since the end of the Second World War and the conflict in Korea, we have seen a profound mutation in the land army. Organized into divisions, into regiments facing off against other corps, other battalions, the wars of the past matched discipline with discipline, rules of the art of war with rules of the art of war; the opposing sides gathered like a reflection in a mirror, except for the color of their uniforms. Later, with the wars of liberation, commonly known as wars of decolonization, those great infantry units, not so far removed from those of Napoleon's armies, had to confront guerrillas in small-scale, less orderly encounters, as partisan factions played a central role in opposing an industrially and numerically superior enemy. Faced with this mutation in the adversary, the great traditional military units have resorted to counterguerrilla commandos. In other words, the regulation soldier has gradually become a partisan, a *guerrillero*, in order to try to beat the guerrillas on their own turf.

This trend toward institutional disintegration, this subversion of the legal armed forces, has not stopped there. Indeed, with the recent development of *international terrorism,* the national armed forces are once again forced to convert: beyond the creation of "rapid deployment task forces" in the United States, France, and elsewhere, preparations are under way for the strategic implementation of a kind of state terrorism, based not only on the organization of small units similar to the rapid-response commandos now traditional among paratroops, marines, or the foreign legion, but on *specialized individuals*, on *logistical couples* comparable to the duo of Rambo and his Vietnamese wife, and especially to the very real couple of Andreas Baader and Gudrun Esslin, in which man and woman again become what they were at the beginning of history: *a war machine.*

Indeed, just as the balance of terror between East and West has contributed to the proliferation of conventional local wars in Asia or Africa for the last thirty years, so the prolonging of nuclear deterrence today contributes to the infinite proliferation of political crimes and individual acts of terrorism. Whether the terrorism is practiced by oppressed minorities or by the police, the effects on the rule of law, civil and international, are devastating, catastrophic. As Rambo tells us: "To survive a war, you become that war."

Already the combatants are no longer the partisans and guerrillas of decolonization, but terrorists of the age of national destabilization. To survive terrorism, according to the logic that applies in this jungle, you *become terrorism*. This becoming terrorism haunts the army as an institution and the military class as a whole, in the East and the West, in the North and the South—whence this year's sudden spate of summit meetings, in Rome, Bonn, and Washington.

For the record, we should also remember the doctrine of free—unrestricted—war, in force for at least a dozen years in the defense organizations of certain Nordic countries, whereby every conscript, every person called up, is transformed into a "partisan."

The future of national defense is no longer solely this "freeing" of war for those resisting an invader superior in number and in armaments. Soon it will be the *freeing of crime*, the training of *mass killers*, paramilitary assassins, licensed criminals assigned to "terrorist units" the way reservists are now called up to serve in the corps of engineers or the infantry. Any technological evolution in light weapons produces this kind of warrior: a soldier-citizen, lone survivor of the great disaffected units of a national army decimated not so much by defeat (colonial or other) as by nonwar, the scientific and technical evolution of the very conditions of economic and political confrontations in the age of nuclear deterrence. The miniaturization of high-performance portable ballistic weapons (assault rifle, rocket launcher) and the sophistication of compact, high-powered explosives combine with the new capabilities of instantaneous telecommunications to produce a new man of war, a sort of *exterminating angel* capable of taking on any enemy at all; a *mass killer* heralded by such recent cinematic productions as James Cameron's *Terminator*, Grand Prix winner at the last Avoriaz Festival. But more than anything else, the mass killer to come is heralded by the evolution of organized crime, *civil terrorism*.

When, in the course of a recent bank holdup in Les Mureaux, gangsters used hand grenades to defend themselves against the police; when, during the robbery of a driving school in Villejuif last month, explosives were used to force the door; when the armored vans of the security service Protecval are attacked with rocket launchers or magnetic mines, how can we fail to see the influence of the methods and means currently employed in Beirut? The practices of political terrorism contaminating the realm of organized crime?

When, on the other hand, we (rightly) worry about the danger of proliferation of atomic weapons and of possible *nuclear terrorism* and then we learn, last winter, via the highly official Pentagon *Military Review*, that American commandos from Detachment A of the Andrew Barracks are currently being trained in Germany in the use of atomic backpacks (miniaturized nuclear rockets), how can we fail to see the profound mutation in legal and illegal violence, the secret kinship, the osmosis, between political and military practices and tools and those of crime? How can we fail to see that, alongside the development of weapons of mass destruction capable of snuffing out the human race, weapons exotically paraded as President Reagan's Strategic Defense Initiative, there also exists an unparalleled development in individual criminal productivity?

Indeed, not only do they now kill the hostages in Beirut, Teheran, or Larnaca, but in the realm of organized crime we are seeing the emergence of new mass murderers, *serial killers* capable of exterminating not just a few people, as before, but hundreds of them, in the manner of a Henry Lee Lucas, who on his own lays claim to 360 victims, the police having already confirmed the figure of 168. Similarly the business with the house in Willseyville, a *micro-extermination camp* harboring a mass grave of twenty-five people, tortured and raped by two individuals, one of whom is a Vietnam veteran.

Closer to home, following the killings in the Bar du Téléphone to which another victim has just been added, we have those of the "Madmen of Brabant," who shot eight people just for the hell of it, including a child of twelve, near Brussels last September during an armed assault on two supermarkets. The gang has chalked up twenty-three dead in all since its first attacks in February 1982.

Under another rubric, one we might call *germ warfare*, note that two Canadians arrested by the FBI at the United States border just a year ago were smuggling in enough botulism and tetanus bacteria to poison a city of three hundred thousand inhabitants. Similarly, under the heading of *chemical warfare*, there was the public poisoner who put cyanide in the jams of the Morinaga company, thumbing his nose at the powerless police of Nagoya and Osaka, Japan.

Hostage-taking and heinous kidnapping in Italy, Lebanon, and elsewhere have become routine; as has the hijacking of public transport and of increasingly imposing vehicles: school buses in Israel, airliners in Jordan and Syria, and even a cruise ship with the pirating of the *Achille Lauro* by a mere four individuals. We are now seeing an extreme escalation in terrorist violence; violence that no longer knows any bounds, any restraint. It will probably end with a city being taken hostage, the sudden hijacking of a metropolis, the tragedy of Beirut providing the model.

How can we fail to see in these latest *acts of state violence* a leveling effect on legitimate violence by illegitimate violence, a victory of terrorism over national and international legitimacy?

After the Israeli air force retaliated against Tunis with F-16s, after the Americans retaliated with F-14s from the aircraft carrier *Saratoga* in the Mediterranean, no matter how some may gloat, *there are only losers:* the Palestinians of the PLO, forced once again to move house in the middle of the peace process with Jordan; the Americans, officially engaged in state terrorism under Reagan, with the assent of the Soviet Union—something which, incidentally, should worry Pentagon analysts; the Israelis, spilling farther and farther beyond their borders since the preventive invasion of Lebanon, sadly misnamed "Peace in Galilee"; and finally the Italians, on the front line ever since the terrorist isobar shifted from the Middle East and settled between Marseilles and Libya, across the Italian peninsula, Sicily, and Tunisia.

The state terrorist attack is never a political success; it is always a failure of public authority, proof of the congenital weakness of legal violence, the violence of law, a right and proper democratic law that attempts to oppose the violence of the unlawful or the arbitrary, the anarchy of individual or collective passions.

If the political state itself gets carried away, if it officially and systematically resorts to crime, it triggers a suicidal process that leads it to its doom, to *military anarchy*, a reign of domestic tyranny for which history has provided many examples from antiquity through recent events in Latin America, with the difficult return to democracy of Argentina or Nicaragua.

"The proximity of serious crime favors man's relationship with the absolute," wrote Rilke. The absolute of right over might, of reason over collective passions: we saw and experienced this during the trial of the Nazis, the monumental Nuremberg trials, as the magistrate and writer Serge Casamayor today testifies.[1]

Surely it will be necessary again to question and judge, as the Russell Tribunal was able to do in its day, the very notion of "crimes against humanity." Crimes not only of terrorist states on the right or left, but also of these *twilight individuals* who are capable on their own of mass exterminations as well as individual genocides, and who are mostly relegated to the news in brief, even though they are monstrous prophets of doom who like to make their victims cry out in the desert—private victims always heralding countless public victims, as the exterminators set the tone for the powers that be.

30 October 1985

Reviewing the elaboration of different types of hardware—weapons, vehicles, and sundry tools, *the materials of war*—whether in the order of strategic or logistical command or in the strictly tactical order of taking an objective (what was once called, in too limiting a way, "the target"), we observe the same tendency toward systematic dematerialization of devices. A dematerialization which, if we are not careful, will soon become a derealization of the aims of war, its processes and politico-military objectives—something the atomic age touched on nearly forty years ago.

From the ancient innovation of the *war machine*, the political and strategic machine of Egypt, Greece, or Rome, right up to the recent appearance of the conditions of possibility for the *declaration-of-war machine*—something that automation, the mastery of computer technology and vectors of rapid delivery, not only allows but requires—the history of armed conflict has been one long series of procedures for dematerializing military tools. This has been part and parcel of the boom in new weaponry: increasingly sophisticated and costly *modes of destruction*, themselves dependent on the economic and social development of the different *modes of production*—agrarian, artisanal, and industrial, right up to the scientific development of nuclear power, though here the military use of fission and fusion energy long preceded their civilian use, a first in the history of natural and synthetic energies. Without citing the long list of technical procedures and politico-military episodes leading up to the development of war software, *the immaterials of war*, one might still sketch in the main lines and high points in this gradual disappearance of the actors and elements once used in battle.

Twelve
The Immaterials of War

There are three aspects to examine. First, the aspect of visual domination, the control of movements and the taking of distant objectives, interdependent with the mastery of information so necessary for avoiding disastrous "surprises." Second, the aspect of command, the hierarchical structure, the flow of practical responsibilities in the engagement of forces, defensive as well as offensive, a system of delegation of power from the commander-in-chief to the commander on the ground and on to the subordinate. Third, armaments, or more precisely *weapons systems*, the logistical combination of means of transport and of destruction, those "vectors of delivery," from the horse and the bow through the muscle-powered artillery of antiquity, to self-propelled cannons, armored vehicles, cruise missiles, and the laser.

If we quickly review the history of military control and surveillance, we note that such "domination" was achieved primarily by the occupation by brute force of natural summits, dominant sites, elevated points of a territory, vantage points from which the scrutinizing gaze could extend far— early means of predicting and anticipating enemy movements, necessary to the preventive mobilization of forces. This provisional military occupation, completed by control of the obligatory transit points—passes, narrow gorges, fords, isthmuses—would then invite settlement by a peasantry that found advantage there because of the protection against attack. These dominant sites would then be fortified, endowed with *watchtowers*, turrets, or abbeys whose bell towers would serve both for observation and to sound the alarm.

Much later, in the seventeenth and eighteenth centuries, with rapid developments in artillery and progress in optics, the telescopic gun sight would gradually take over this preventive function, adding to the natural or constructed high point the "long view" (field glasses) or telescope that effortlessly homes in on whatever keeps its distance: the first immaterial communications tool, coming after the smoke signal and well before the installation of Chappe's telegraph, the wireless telephone, or television.

In the nineteenth century, notably during the American Civil War, this function of preventive domination would be assured by observation balloons carrying aeronauts equipped with cameras. "Military kites" would also be used, equipped with box cameras triggered by a cord. With the First World War and particularly the Second, the early twentieth century would see the reconnaissance plane, armed with a high-resolution movie camera, take over from towers and observation balloons. More importantly, with radar and sonar we would see the invention of electronic imaging, the first significant dematerialization of a system of audiovisual surveillance achieved by waves, electromagnetic radiation, the vibrations of an electronic ether. Finally, during the 1960s, with the conquest of space, observation and telecommunications satellites would perfect Galileo's telescope by allowing us to contemplate not the stars anymore but the Earth, an earth where no important movement can now be carried out without a screen lighting up somewhere, an indicator on some electronic console . . . All this in anticipation of the manning of permanent orbital platforms, *early-warning satellites*, sidereal lookouts for the Star Wars slated for the end of the century!

If we take a similar look at the historical evolution of weaponry and the different weapons systems, from the old hand-held weapons (knife, broadsword, sword, etc.) or projectiles (stone, arrow, javelin, etc.) up to contemporary nuclear armaments, we observe the same trend.

If hand-held weapons have never ceased *getting bigger* over the centuries, the better to reach an enemy that keeps himself at a distance and often on horseback, projectiles have never ceased *being propelled ever farther*, with ever-greater destructive effect, right up to neutron bombs with their *enhanced radiation*.

From the Roman *pilum* (heavy javelin) and Greek or Roman muscle-powered artillery using the natural elasticity of stretched cables to project blocks of stone some few hundred meters, from the short bows of prehistoric times right up to the crossbow and, via the English longbows of the Battle of Agincourt, to the harquebus, the musket, the carbine, and the contemporary automatic rifle, we observe a constant shift: from muscular energy right up to nuclear energy, via the use of chemical explosives, the fabled gunpowder that brought a considerable increase in the range and pace of firing, causing the gradual disappearance of ramparts and massive shields as well as the disintegration of combat formations into smaller, less vulnerable units. *A dematerialization that has thus affected both the weapon and its display*, the fort and the fortified town, the troop and the trooper. Whence the necessity for dissimulation, camouflage, and today lures, those *electronic countermeasures* alone capable of safeguarding against the impact of missiles with "homing devices." New weapons, capable of taking their objectives by themselves; "self-guided" missiles belonging to the tellingly named *fire and forget* weapons system.

From now on, in fact, man will no longer be protected by the thickness of stone or reinforced concrete, nor by the hardness of armor plating, any more than by the extreme distance that separates him from his adversary. He will be protected by the jamming of enemy guidance systems, at which point the electronic war catches up with chemical and germ warfare—the innovation of asphyxiating gases and especially of those debilitating products, delivered by aerosol, that are capable of attacking the will and nervous system of combatants, much as enemy missile guidance systems are crippled.

Finally, the long scientific and technical development of cannon range, from a few hundred meters to the current tens of kilometers (from forty to one hundred kilometers for very long-range guns), as well as the constant increase in the initial velocity of the projectiles and their rate of fire (up to six thousand rounds a minute for electrified weapons) and the invention of rockets, intercontinental ballistic missiles—to say nothing of the laser weapon (directed-energy weapon) working at the speed of light, or 300,000 kilometers a second—have contributed to locking the protagonists of armed combat into a decisive face-off that is no longer the province of the political and military leaders of both camps, but essentially of their weapons systems. A warning system and an electronic protection system for defense, an instantaneous firing system for offense, which leads us to the last of the three aspects named above, no longer involving just the *dematerialization* of the means of destruction, but also the gradual *depersonalization* of the chain of command; a loss of properly human political will in favor of compulsory automation of decision-making, the imminent arrival of this *declaration-of-war machine*, a supposedly transpolitical machine capable of supplanting the supreme decision-maker, the head of state. This is the *doomsday machine*, on the drawing board now for nearly ten years, the brainchild of computer scientists specializing in "expert systems" . . .

In going over the steps in this awesome mutation of power, from tribal wars up to the general staff of modern conflicts, via the strategies of antiquity and the great captains of the Middle Ages, we observe the same concentration of decision-making power. Where early warriors each enjoyed a very broad autonomy and great personal responsibility due to the overwhelming importance of tactics in conflicts that were little more than "manhunts," the combatants of the phalanxes and legions of antiquity had to quickly submit to a strict discipline, one connected to the burgeoning of strategy, deriving from the necessities of government and defense of the city-state.

Through the vicissitudes of the history of the West and the empires of Europe, this requirement of the political economy of war grew continually, with the rise of the nation-states and the great armed confrontations that ensued. The birth of the general staff should be credited to the enormous maintenance problems and difficulties met by ministers and superior officers faced with constant growth in the number of combatants: from some tens of thousands once upon a time, to some hundreds of thousands, to, finally, several million individuals forming the battalions essential to victory in the mass war. This situation would lead, in the nineteenth century and especially in the twentieth, to the primacy of *logistics*, the establishment of military-industrial and scientific complexes, and the commitment of a larger and larger share of national resources to research and development of new arms in peacetime.

The general staff of the army in 1914, the general staff of the group of armies (1939 to 1945), with MacArthur in the Pacific and Eisenhower as Allied commander-in-chief of the European front—this gigantism foreshadowed the decline of the old military hierarchy; a decline soon pressed by the power of nuclear weapons and even more so by the rapidity of their delivery: a few hours for the airborne bomb of Hiroshima, less than an hour for intercontinental ballistic missiles (ICBMs), a few minutes for intermediate-range rockets (SS 20, Pershing II), and finally a few seconds for the short-range missiles currently based in Central Europe.

Dematerialization of armaments, *depersonalization* of command, *derealization* of the aims of war: the question currently posed by the "immaterials of war" is central. Having accepted, in the course of past centuries, the infinite delegation of political and military powers and their tyrannical concentration, are we about to accept the delegation of the *ultima ratio*, the decision to declare war, to *expert systems* that are alone capable of reacting in "real time" to other devices of the same kind? An insane coupling of systems of detection and nuclear release belonging to opposing camps and likely to unleash the apocalypse . . . In fact, all things considered, the apocalypse is no longer nuclear war, but the positive or negative response that we will bring to the question of automation.

15 November 1984

Automation does not eliminate the possibility of human error, it transfers this possibility of error from the action phase to the design and development phase.
—Andrew Stratton

One of the most enigmatic aspects of technology concerns the temporal regimes of the objects, materials, and assemblages produced. Everyone agrees that the "components" of our natural environment comprise and combine relative durations that man learned long ago to perceive and then to control: seasonal rhythms, cyclical systems, specific durations, etc. In the realm of contemporary technologies, professional experience has also made it possible to control variations due to aging and structural wear and tear. Chemistry has also facilitated our understanding of the infinitesimal mutations time produces in the elements. At the level of advanced technologies, by contrast, it seems we are seeing a reversal that affects human capacities for control and even for simple apprehension of phenomena. On the one hand, the effects induced by very long-term processes (contamination, irreversible pollution) exceed our capacity for monitoring and statistical approximation. On the other hand, the general spread of automation reduces the power of those directly in charge to implement and maintain processes, pushing this responsibility back to the planning stages, to a designer-decision-maker who, despite computer technology and simulation devices, has no means of evaluation. Last but not least, this rarefaction of control affects the temporal regime of the human decision-maker. After the now-classic phases of *mechanization-motorization-automation* comes the last phase: *cybernation*. From this moment on, phenomena that happen *here*, in common space, no longer happen *now*, in common time, but in an *other time* over which no one has any power, despite the tragic illusions of computer technology.

This invention of an uncertain time, a veritable *technological beyond*, is not an inevitable consequence of scientific and technological progress; it is largely the result of the evolution of the politics of defense. In the age-old doctrine of national defense, preventive measures were taken against *an enemy* located *beyond the border*; but with the doctrine of security, we guard ourselves against *threats*—threats to the nation that result less from adverse demographics than from the boom in war industries. The fear is thus no longer of a visible and concrete adversary geographically located and politically defined; it is primarily the fear of the capabilities of that adversary's hardware and the delivery power of his most destructive weapons (planes, rockets, submarines). *The beyond is no longer the beyond of a territory, of a political space around which it is appropriate to build ramparts; it is the beyond of real time, the beyond of a specifically human space-time*, from which we are progressively exiling ourselves.

Listen to General Gallois, one of the promoters of French nuclear strategy: "Our retaliatory forces must be given a quasi-automatic power of implementation. The quasi-inevitability of reaction to a threat is indispensable."

We are compelled to note that such a military option sooner or later leads to the elimination of human intervention from the loop of detection-designation-pursuit-engagement, and thus to our abandoning ourselves to *the inevitability of a cybernetic process*, with all the fallout this presupposes at the level of national and international politics.

Note certain eyewitness accounts of the recent war in the Falklands. A British war correspondent recounts: "You don't hear anything coming, then suddenly, you're in the middle of an incredible fireworks display. When you hear the noise of the planes, they are already long gone and the attack is over."

The account of an Argentinean pilot: "We don't have time to get scared, everything happens in a few seconds. The sight lights up just in front of the windshield, everything is ready for the computer to do its work. It's the computer that has the last word."

And finally, the tale of the commander of the destroyer *Sheffield*, sunk by a single missile: "The attack was like lightning. In this war of missiles you only get a few seconds, or a few fractions of a second, to react. . . . It's horrifying. This is a new war the experts know nothing about." That last phrase, *a new war the experts know nothing about*, illustrates perfectly the revolution going on in modes of destruction: *the doctrine of production has replaced the doctrine of use on the battlefield.* The funeral home's computer already has the last word . . .

For if there is no more doctrine of arms use to teach at war school, if the experts know nothing about this new war, this is because *the time allocated to decision-making is now insufficient*. The slogan of the "smart missiles" (homing devices, cruise missiles, etc.)—*fire and forget*—signifies a transfer in human decision-making from the stage of action and use in the field to the stage of design and military-industrial programming. What is being automated here is no longer simply the "means of destruction" (automatic weapons, self-programmed projectiles); it is first and foremost *the conduct of war*, of a war more often than not undeclared, you will notice.

The theoretical war of military-scientific design thus gradually supersedes the great maneuvers of war in the field.

If, as Lenin once explained, "strategy is the choice of points where force is to be applied," we are now forced to conclude that there is no longer a strategy of military maneuver, only *a logistical strategy of military-scientific programming*, independent of the various political powers, in the East as in the West.

The Falklands War, like the wars in the Middle East, thus illustrates yet again the regressive nature of advanced technologies. The declared lack of any doctrine of use for the new means of destruction points up the trend: bypassing geopolitics and geostrategy in favor of logistics, a logistics on the way to becoming "global" not only because of the range of the new over-the-horizon weapons and the long operating range of the missiles, but especially because of the temporal regimes of the very latest weapons systems.

As Andrew Stratton explained ten years back: "The progress in missile exchange risks reducing to nothing the time left to the human being to decide to intervene in the system."

In this dire perspective, *compulsory automation becomes the transfer accident of advanced technologies.* Going to war now means simply going over to the accident of forced automation: the transfer of responsibility (human, political) from the stage of decision-making on the battlefield to the stage of industrial and economic programming.

Thus, war goes back to basics, back to its essence. By a secret osmosis that affects, or will shortly affect, the entire mode of production of weapons systems (design, programming, manufacture, use), war seeps into the heart of the command apparatus (political, geopolitical, geostrategic). Indeed, if "war" is no longer officially declared, as was the case in the Falklands or in Lebanon, and if "the enemy" is rejected in favor of "threats" (direct or indirect) to national interests, this is simply because *relative war* has replaced erstwhile *relative peace* and because the true act of war is expressed less by a declaration of hostilities between one nation and another than by the international development of a "mode of destruction"—

this automation of "means" that is a prelude to the automation of "ends," in which the war machine suddenly becomes a *declaration-of-war machine*, a doomsday machine that will see the very possibility of any political choice between war and peace fly through our fingers.

This apocalyptic situation explains the timeliness of the current debate over unilateral renunciation of the nuclear first-strike doctrine, a debate which, in the United States, has brought together personalities no more "pacifist" than Robert McNamara, McGeorge Bundy, George Kennan, and Gerard Smith, a former negotiator of the SALT I accords.

Today, if it is no longer politically necessary to opt for war or its conduct in the field, this is because "pure war" has long ago been declared, with deterrence, in the field of knowledge at the heart of military-industrial and scientific design.

Indeed, with the acquisition of a speed that precludes the pauses indispensable to political and military leaders for reflection and decision-making, *the concept of war has become autonomous and war has become automated*—just like the weapons and vehicles that have long enabled war to extend to any part of the globe.

"Swiftness is the essence of war," the strategist Sun Tzu wrote a long time ago . . . Victims of this now quintessential war, made redundant by the quasi-instantaneity of response times, the "politician" and the "military man" can only regress: intervening at the stage of weapons design and their on-the-spot deployment. Whence the proliferation of U.S.-Soviet bilateral talks in Geneva on strategic arms reduction, on Euromissiles, and recently on the reduction of these same arms and preparation of the future START accords. Meanwhile we all look forward to the great international conference that will finally set a *speed limit for war*—not just the control and end of the "arms race," but this time *an end to arming the advanced-technologies race;* a sort of scientific and industrial armistice, an interlude designed to stop the unpredictable ravages of pure war, the forced automation of means as well as ends, before it is too late.

In a recent interview, Lucien Sfez, former chief of staff in a ministry of the Mauroy government, voiced his surprise over the pace of decision-making within the administration: "The only thing that amazed me," he said, "was how fast decisions were made. I was interested in memory, in time, but always in the long haul, continuous time, no doubt because I came from the university system where there is never any urgency. But in a ministry everything is very short: decisions take five minutes, a quarter of an hour, an hour. The long term means a week."

This testimony is invaluable insofar as it conveys the extreme swiftness of *civilian* decision-making. But in matters of *military* emergency, the long term means an hour!

With the recent progress in ballistics, everything is now performed in very short order: a few minutes in the medium term; a few seconds, meaning a few fractions of a second, in the short term. We should recall here that the doctrine of surprise nuclear attack requires that to reach their target, missiles must be fired even before those of the enemy can have left the ground. The response time is now so short that, in a moment of international crisis, war and peace are decided by computer: this is the *launch-on-warning system.*

Having reached this point in history, as expiatory victims of a general state of emergency, we find renunciation of the doctrine of nuclear "first strike" a preliminary responsible gesture toward reaching a "military-scientific armistice." There is no longer any question of seeking *to gain time* through the growing sophistication of machines, vectors of delivery; or of improving nuclear reaction and hoping *to win by surprise.* We can see fairly well now that the only surprise would have to be this sudden mutation of the old "war machine" into a *declaration-of-war machine*, a sudden-death machine over which we would no longer have any power.

Finally, the human error involved in military-scientific programming would surely lie in underestimating the invisible violence of the delivery speed of vectors (rocket, missile, laser) in favor of the spectacular violence of the atomic explosive alone. This is the tragic illusion of nuclear deterrence—deterrence in use of the absolute explosive, not deterrence in the development of the implosive, the hyperspeed that can, by depriving us of the time necessary for reflection, deprive us once and for all of responsibility for our fate. Speaking of which, remember also that the Pentagon has declared that it will soon be capable of carrying out instant nuclear attacks and that, since 1982, the United States has had a U.S. Air Force Strategic Space Command, designed to prepare the putting into orbit of an *early-warning satellite* capable of providing American defense systems with a greater margin of reaction time in case of a nuclear alert.

So today the inevitable means not so much the destructive power of the atom as the power of instantaneous delivery; a "delivery" that will soon, if we don't watch out, deliver us from all power—without a real war ever having started.

The countdown has in fact begun. In a few months, a few years at most, there will no longer be time to intervene; real time will have imploded.

Paul Virilio, Paris

Calling Card

1. Ecclesiasticus 39:20. The full verse is: "The works of all flesh are before Him, and nothing can be hid from His eyes. He seeth from everlasting to everlasting; and there is nothing wonderful before Him" (39:19–20).

2. Herman Melville, "A Canticle," in *Battle-Pieces and Aspects of the War* (1866; New York: Thomas Yoseloff, 1964), pp. 128–129.

3. Erri de Luca, *Libération*, 30 May 1996.

4. Walter Benjamin, "Theses on the Philosophy of History," in Benjamin, *Illuminations*, ed. Hannah Arendt, trans. Harry Zohn (New York: Harcourt, Brace and World, 1968), p. 259; italics added and translation modified.

one The Big Night

1. The passages in italics are taken from Pierre Mac Orlan's *Fanny Hill*. It was also in the seventeenth century that the systematic illumination of Europe's shores began, with the construction of the first permanent lighthouses.

2. Shakespeare, *Hamlet*, 3.3.15–17.

3. *"Tolerant neighborhoods,"* the old *red-light districts*, modern *offshore* areas, where all the outcasts of an era take up residence.

4. Hannah Arendt, *The Life of the Mind* (London: Secker and Warburg, 1978), vol. 1, pp. 176–177; modified.

5. Michael Heim, *The Metaphysics of Virtual Reality* (New York: Oxford University Press, 1993).

6. Comments made at the MILIA (Marché international de l'édition et des nouveaux médias), Cannes, 15 February 1996.

7. Plato, *The Republic*, trans. H. D. P. Lee (London: Penguin, 1958), book 9, p. 348; translation modified.

8. See the Big Bang affair in cosmology or the new "philosophical vogue" launched by the media, with its panoply of metaphysical bestsellers: J.-C. Bennet, *La Conscience expliquée;* Luc Ferry, *L'Homme-Dieu ou le sens de la vie;* Jean Daniel, *Dieu est-il fanatique?,* etc. But also, as a tragic echo: the burning of churches (U.S.), the destruction of places of worship (ex-Yugoslavia), the massacre of members of religious orders (Africa), satanic gatherings, the growing number of eschatological and criminal sects, the profanation of graves and corpses. A host of crimes that elude previous explanations—political, racist, or other.

two **The Avant-Garde of Forgetting**

1. "Larry King, roi sur CNN," *Libération,* 9 June 1994.

four **The Imbalance of Terror**

1. See Bob Woodward, *The Commanders* (New York: Simon and Schuster, 1991).

2. Marcel Gauchet interviewed by Marie Chaudey and Raphaël Poitevin, *La Vie,* November 1991.

3. Seneca, "Letter to Lucilius" in *Moral Letters.*

five **The Near-Death Experience**

1. René Descartes, *Meditations,* trans. Elizabeth S. Haldane and G. R. T. Ross (Chicago: Encyclopaedia Britannica, 1952), Meditation 11, p. 81.

2. Michel Foucault, *The Order of Things* (New York: Vintage, 1973), p. xxiii.

3. The NDE takes its inspiration from the work of one Raymond A. Moody, whose first book, *Life after Life* (New York: Bantam Books, 1976), sold more than ten million copies!

4. Foucault, *The Order of Things,* p. 387.

six **A Glimpse**

1. Irvin Rock, *The Logic of Perception* (Cambridge: MIT Press, 1983), pp. 181–187.

2. Jean Oury, *Création et schizophrénie* (Paris: Galilée, 1989).

eight **The Accident Museum**

1. On this theme, see Pierre Thuillier, "Les Origines de l'anti-science," *La Recherche*, February 1986.

2. In this domain, note Sacha Ketoff's groundbreaking exhibition "Air Crash" (Galerie Lacloche, June 1978).

3. As in the case of the exhibition "Les Immatériaux" (Pompidou Center, spring 1985).

ten **The Fire Tomorrow**

1. James Baldwin, "The Fire Next Time," in *The Price of the Ticket: Collected Non-Fiction 1948–1985* (London: Michael Joseph, 1985), p. 369.

eleven **Mass Murderer**

1. Serge Casamayor, *Nuremberg, 1945: La Guerre en procès* (Paris: Stock, 1985).